DoCoMo

JAPAN'S WIRELESS TSUNAMI

DoCoMo
JAPAN'S WIRELESS TSUNAMI

How One Mobile Telecom Created a
New Market and Became a Global Force

JOHN BECK
AND
MITCHELL WADE

AMACOM
American Management Association
New York • Atlanta • Brussels • Buenos Aires • Chicago • London • Mexico City
San Francisco • Shanghai • Tokyo • Toronto • Washington, D. C.

Special discounts on bulk quantities of AMACOM books are available to corporations, professional associations, and other organizations. For details, contact Special Sales Department, AMACOM, a division of American Management Association, 1601 Broadway, New York, NY 10019.
Tel.: 212-903-8316   Fax: 212-903-8083
Web site: www.amacombooks.org

This publication is designed to provide accurate and authoritative information in regard to the subject matter covered. It is sold with the understanding that the publisher is not engaged in rendering legal, accounting, or other professional service. If legal advice or other expert assistance is required, the services of a competent professional person should be sought.

Library of Congress Cataloging-in-Publication Data

Beck, John C.
  DoCoMo : Japan's wireless tsunami / John C. Beck and Mitchell E. Wade.
      p. cm.
Includes bibliographical references and index.
  ISBN 0-8144-0753-6
  1. DoCoMo—History. 2. Cellular telephone services
industry—Japan—History. I. Wade, Mitchell E. II. Title.
  HE9715.J3 B435 2002
  384.3'06'552—dc21   2002008312

Printing number
10 9 8 7 6 5 4 3 2 1

For Roger
—JB

For my parents
—MW

CONTENTS

INTRODUCTION

We have a confession to make: This isn't the book we thought we were going to write. And if you're looking for a safe, detailed history of an exceptional company, this isn't it.

Let us explain. NTT DoCoMo *is* a truly exceptional company. Largely unknown outside Japan, it has created more wealth in recent years than almost any other company in the world. (The Stern Stewart Wealth Added Index [WAI] compares share-price increases and dividends to the cost of equity for 5069 firms worldwide, from June 1996 to June 2001. DoCoMo is the only Asian firm in the WAI top ten, and one of only three from outside the United States.)

Originally spun off from a hidebound bureaucracy, DoCoMo was the kind of startup that might simply have faded away. Instead, it has become a true global superpower. It has over 30 million paying Internet customers—as many as America Online—but got there five times faster. Its technology is a full generation ahead of anything in the United States or Europe. And it is rapidly acquiring stakes in every major global market. Insiders believe this Japanese powerhouse could dominate the new economy, just as Sony and Toyota have dominated the old one.

So the elements are there for the book you might expect: a classic (if conventional) high-tech success story. What's more, this is clearly a success story that matters, truly, to the entire industrialized world. For some time now, just about every telecom you can think of has been investing and positioning and preparing for the Big Mobile Commerce Boom. And many other businesses have been watching closely, because mobile data is one of the very few things that seem capable of bringing the good times back. It's the economic grail, or at least one of them: a disruptive information technology that begins once more to drive growth in stock prices, employment, wages, and housing—just about all the markets that matter. But the Boom hasn't really happened yet...except in Japan. When you look a little closer, what that really means is that it has only happened, so far, for one company: DoCoMo.

So anyone who cares about recapturing boom times—anyone who wants to see the tech sector come roaring back—needs to know DoCoMo's story. Certainly, all the players who are now investing for this wireless future (as well as the skeptics not investing) need to know. Yet the one company that has really pulled this off has remained almost an unknown. Those who do care about wireless know something about its success. But most of them write it off with explanations that, stripped of their camouflage, boil down to "Oh, those wacky Japanese!"

To us, that seems like a mistake, and that's why we began the book. John had lived in Japan, consulted all over the world, and taught international business for twenty years.* He knew that Japan was on a different continent, not on a different planet. Mitch, who had spent the same twenty years looking at how people actually use information, knew that driving the adoption of a complex new technology was getting harder just as the real-world impact of those technologies (or at least their potential impact) was growing much larger. And both of us were conducting wireless-commerce research at Accenture's Institute for Strategic Change, a think tank focused on ideas that lead to immediate management action.

From this perspective, it seemed obvious that DoCoMo's success really matters. We felt strongly that no company that had succeeded so thoroughly—especially in a field with so much intense and skillful competition—could be ignored. After all, DoCoMo had accumulated that AOL-size user base, in a market where paying users were scarce. It was reaching milestones, such as a market cap that, for a time, made it the second largest company in the world. Only a few years old, it

---

*Throughout this book, the two authors will be referring to each other by their first names, John and Mitch.

was big enough to start buying significant stakes in companies like AT&T Wireless. Given all that, the lessons from its core success, no matter how Japan-specific, would surely be of use to other competitors. Who knows? They might even hold the key to starting up that Big Mobile Commerce Boom.

So with the generous support, unflagging enthusiasm, and matchless industry knowledge of Masakatsu Mori and Chikatomo Hoda at Accenture, we began to study the case of DoCoMo. Colleagues there, led by Meiko Ueyama and Junko Ohhira, provided Japanese-language documents, detailed analytic material, and company expertise that simply can't be found anywhere else. Then Yuiichiro "Pat" Kuwahata, DoCoMo's head of International Public Relations, with the blessing of CEO Keiji Tachikawa, managed to line up interviews for us with all of the top executives in the firm. These in-depth discussions provided us with unprecedented access; we knew we had a chance to crack the code—to really understand why DoCoMo's i-mode service had swept its entire national market by storm at exactly the moment when wireless data offerings worldwide were being met with a resounding yawn.

We began our research looking for strategies, tactics, technologies, details of execution and leadership—all the ingredients that case studies traditionally focus on. And that's what we found, at first. But once we got behind the DoCoMo curtain, and began to hear directly and at length from the people who had actually made this success happen, we discovered a surprise:

In the end, this huge techno-success story is all about feelings.

The triumph of DoCoMo is *not* mainly about engineering, or the right legacy infrastructure, or backing the winning technical standard. It's *not* mainly about pricing the service wisely, or guaranteeing distribution, or staying close to customers. Even though DoCoMo is a very Japanese company, its triumph is *not* really about dedication and efficiency. All those are part of the story, of course. But many competing companies have done quite well on all those dimensions. In the end, what sets DoCoMo apart is *passion*.

That's a surprise to many, who know only a little about Japan. But those who have experienced Japan more deeply realize that feelings are central—as central, in fact, as in our seemingly "warmer" Western culture. In one of the first American books written about Japanese business, *Japan's Managerial System*, Harvard Business School professor Michael Yoshino explained that the basic building block of Japanese social structure was *giri* (obligation or duty). But a society based only on duty would be too hard to endure, so a complementary concept emerged: *ninjo*. The term can be defined literally as "sympathy" or "kindness," but in a culture where good and evil are determined almost completely by social context, ninjo takes a much more important place. It has come to mean "human feeling," and it is the glue that holds Japan together.

We would argue that Japan is not alone in needing this glue; almost every society, almost every business, almost every person trying to make things happen in the real world, could profit from a little more ninjo. Looking closely at DoCoMo's performance, we suspect that the smart, dedicated, hardworking business culture here in the United States would actually become even more productive with a little less attention to the obvious aspects of creating value, and a little more attention to passion.

In our research at DoCoMo, the role of human feelings was obvious. Once the key figures began sharing their experience with it, there was no denying the point: Passions are vital. This very young company faced the huge challenge of creating a mass market for wireless data (and, before that, the substantial challenge of creating a national market for cell phones at a time when Japanese customers just weren't interested). They succeeded beyond anyone's expectations because the right people in the company had the right mix of powerful, human emotions—and proved extremely skillful at managing them. DoCoMo used passions to lead its own creative and competitive efforts, to lead the market, and, ultimately, to lead a global industry.

These findings force us to propose a radical, almost embarrassing idea: In managing your business, human passions matter. A lot. More than any of us admit, and certainly more than we act on. (And we are deliberately excluding the obvious place for feelings—the only place many managers think about them—which is marketing and advertising.) Feelings are worth paying attention to, in your daily management, in choosing what company or group or project to work on, and in selecting technologies to back or companies to invest in. Want to get a great job, avoid a layoff, stay in the good graces of your board, keep a key customer, or get a good deal from a supplier? Skill, talent, profitability, quality, responsiveness, and a slew of other business issues are vital. But lots of individuals and companies can do comparably well in these areas.

Usually the decisions that most affect your career and the success of your company come down to questions like this: Does my boss like me? Does the board trust me? Will customers call me, before calling a competitor, because they just prefer talking to me? Would my supplier be willing to shave a percentage point off the product price just to continue our working relationship?

Reflecting on the research presented here, we believe that a company that understands the power of human passions, and manages those passions in its customers, its employees, and its leaders, will create value faster than its competitors.

DoCoMo is a fantastic example. Here's a company that went from essentially zero to over $30 billion in revenues, without major acquisitions, in only a few years—mainly because in several key areas it tapped into the power of feelings. In a floundering national economy, in a sector where billions have been invested for disappointing returns, in a product category that most customers don't yet understand, DoCoMo launched what is surely the most successful new product in history. By the time i-mode was barely two years old, it was carried by a third of the adults in its home market. Although there are extremely capable wireless competitors in Europe and the United States, to say nothing of Asia, none has matched this feat. So far, none has even come close.

We believe that the only way to really understand that success—and find ways to emulate it in your own business—is to explore the passions that DoCoMo has used to lead. These include the very personal feelings of the company's:

■ *Customers*—their love for one another, their passion for freedom, and their excitement at being in on a shared social phenomenon.

■ *Senior Leaders*—whose passion defined their management style, and who used those passions to inspire the company they led.

■ *Key Creative Employees*—the unlikely people who basically invented i-mode. DoCoMo couldn't have done it without them. And they couldn't have done it without some very particular emotions—enabled by those above them—that don't usually show up in corporate annual reports.

■ *Managers and Staff at Every Level*—the human beings who together make up so much of any company's corporate culture. To DoCoMo, these people brought exactly the passion it takes to create a phenomenal run of good luck.

■ *Next Generation of Leaders*—supplying DoCoMo with the one passion that can help the company surmount its two greatest challenges. This feeling, already commented on by business partners in the West, is crucial in determining how much farther DoCoMo's success can extend.

As you can see, this book is very much about people and passions. But we assure you, it is not "touchy-feely." After all, it is real data—including the thoughtful comments of very serious, successful, and businesslike people—that brought us (with great surprise) to these conclusions. And we accepted them ourselves only after extensive reading and analysis. So while we will tell you DoCoMo's inside story—revealing these passions—we will also share the intellectual underpinnings. Every chapter includes analytic information, based on both well-founded theory and practical experience, to help understand why passion, and specifically these particular passions, should be so important, not just for DoCoMo, but for other firms in other industries. And we never lose sight of the "so what?" question. Each chapter ends with concrete actions you can take to convert the lessons of DoCoMo into extraordinary performance for your own firm.

After all, passion is great...but why get all worked up over something you can't act on? We believe that a look inside DoCoMo will give you some great stories, some new ideas, and some insight into the emerging wireless economy. But much more important, we believe that the core lessons of this story will help you turn your own passions into business success.

CHAPTER ONE

Love

"Love and work are viewed as totally separate,
yet work without love is dead."
—MARTA ZAHAYKEVICH

BUSINESS CASES aren't romance novels. Things begin, and end, with the numbers. If there's a story behind those numbers, it's supposed to be a military epic: brilliant generals, clashing armies, risky maneuvers. DoCoMo's story has all that and more. But at its core, DoCoMo's success depends on a love story. Somewhere, mixed in with the systematic analysis of corporate strategy, the technical innovation of engineering, the analytically derived emotion of marketing, and the ruthless efficiency of operations, the i-mode team sparked a love affair.

But we're getting ahead of ourselves. Why should anyone care about this particular love story? Because it created success for Japan exactly where every industrial nation needs it—and exactly where efforts in the United States and Europe have met only failure. *With i-mode, DoCoMo made commerce on the mobile Internet compelling—so compelling that it is fast becoming universal throughout Japan.* Even there, in an economy plagued by recession for ten years or more, the result has been the kind of tech-fueled boom that the entire developed world is now praying for. By delivering mobile Internet access that people actually use for new kinds of business, DoCoMo cre-

1

ated enormous value. Its market capitalization shot from just under 2 trillion yen (about $16 billion) to almost 45 trillion yen (almost $400 billion) in less than a year. It captured 30 million paying Internet customers, about as many as AOL, in one fifth of the time. And it earned the chance—the top seed, really—to become a major player in the nascent (almost dormant) market for wireless data here in the United States, to say nothing of Europe and the rest of Asia. It did all that with i-mode, a system that turns the pedestrian cell phone into a personal network connection. Always with you, always on, i-mode invites its millions of paying subscribers not only to send messages to one another, but to download and pay for!—information. It delivers them news, entertainment, and other content exactly when and where they want it. And it gives all kinds of businesses a direct channel to the consumer at the point where a sale is really likely. Technically, much of that is possible now on the wireless Web services marketed outside Japan. But, as anyone who has tried those services knows, most are not yet ready for prime time. DoCoMo's i-mode is not only ready; it is a runaway success, a blockbuster hit. *That's* why the story matters.

This is a big story. Only a complex set of passions could give DoCoMo the explosive energy needed to reach its current, unchallenged position. Later, we're going to tell you about all of the passions. But this chapter focuses on the emotion that started it all: love.

What's Love Got to Do with It?

Launching a new product, especially an info-tech product, has gotten tougher in the past few years. And it doesn't look like it is going to get better any time soon. With no small irony, the principal culprit has been revealed as *information technology itself*. As John* and our colleague, Tom Davenport, explained in *The Attention Economy*,[1] when information becomes cheap and plentiful, something else becomes scarce: attention. That's a resource that many of us implicitly assume is free, or at least cheap. And for a long while, for most consumers,

---

*As mentioned in the Introduction, the two authors will refer to each other by their first names.

it was. But we need to change that almost invisible assumption, because the reality is now completely different. When the average grocery store holds 40,000 SKUs, yet each family buys only about 150; when there are 300,000 new books published worldwide each year; when hundred–e-mail days are common and we find ourselves fast-forwarding through *everything*...well, we're not exaggerating when we say that attention is *the* scarce resource. That has implications throughout business.

"Don't worry about people stealing

your ideas. If your ideas are any good, you'll

have to ram them down people's throats."

—ATTRIBUTED TO HOWARD AIKEN

One of the most ironic implications, though, is that it's tough for innovations—even absolutely great new ideas—to be adopted. New ideas have always had a tough road. In olden days (say, the 1970s), a cool new product might have been considered or even tried, then perhaps rejected as risky, unfamiliar, or just plain weird. Now, though, its most likely fate is much worse. Innovations seldom get to the thrill of true customer rejection; instead, they are simply ignored, lost in the flood of information that washes over us all.

Loving I-mode

So when you see a new product take off like i-mode has, reaching 30 million users—almost a third of the population of Japan!!!—without even slowing down, you have the chance to learn from a rare and valuable phenomenon: a historic triumph of adoption. In a market full of electronic gadgets, i-mode somehow captured the passion of millions of customers, then sustained and leveraged that passion to build new habits—and an enormous business in an entirely new category. That feat made the company a huge pile of money. Emulating it might do the same for you.

FIGURE 1-1. Monthly i-mode user growth in Japan: 2000 to 2002.

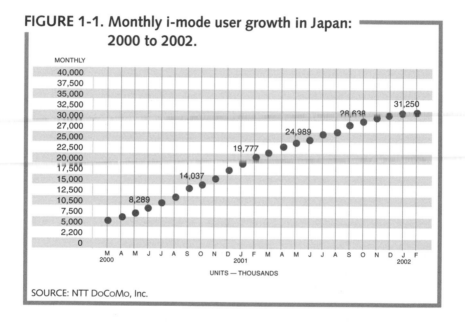

SOURCE: NTT DoCoMo, Inc.

That's where love comes in. No, not your passion, or anyone's, for money. The way DoCoMo created this world-class feat of adoption—in a market where billions of dollars have been invested worldwide, with disappointing results—was to spark a love affair. Why? Because, whether they knew it or not, they had to. Like any new product, i-mode needed to break through the competition for consumers' time, attention, and money. Like any new *kind of* product, it also had to overcome barriers of apathy, suspicion, and fear.

Think of it on the human level. In i-mode's first three years on the market, 30 million consumers purchased the handset and signed up for service. Before i-mode came along, almost none of these people struggled with a surplus of time and cash. Virtually all were getting along quite nicely without a next-generation cell phone, and certainly without mobile Internet access. And most, if they bought i-mode, faced some risk of:

- Being embarrassed at spending a lot of money on a gadget that didn't turn out to be valuable

- Being seen owning and trying to operate a device they weren't familiar with

- Wasting time learning the tricks needed to use a new system

- Discovering that no one else wanted i-mode, and worst

- Being forced to admit that they made an expensive mistake.

Something for the Pain

In theory, the way you overcome all those barriers—the risks, the competition, the inertia—is by delivering rational economic value. You offer consumers enough convenience, or savings, or other measurable, practical good things, and they in turn buy your product. That's certainly true, as far as it goes. In a steady-state world, where people know and understand their options, including your product, it might even work. But for customers in our post-modern consumer economy—with their basic needs long since satisfied; with technology creating more new products than anyone can even know about, much less sample; with attention by far their scarcest resource—that kind of value is not enough. To successfully introduce any package of information and technology, you need a lot more. You need to touch people where they live. You need passion. You need, for example, love.

And love is what i-mode delivered. For millions of consumers, it tapped into deeply felt needs, desires, and wishes. As is often true with new product types, customers themselves weren't sure why they were taking the plunge. But if you look carefully, you can see it: In one form or another, the love was there. As in many love stories, it was tangled with two other complex and powerful elements: constant and unpredictable change, on the one hand, and the eternal mystery of why we humans do what we do, on the other. Consider the following.

The Tale of Two Sisters

"I think you're talking to the wrong person."

A mutual friend had suggested that Yasuko Sato would be a good example of an Internet phone user: Japan's new wired (well, wireless) generation. She obviously didn't agree.

To almost any global businessperson, Yasuko is impressive—almost the emblem of modern Japan—and easy to identify with. Poised and attractive, she is clearly intelligent, hardworking, and dedicated to achievement. Yasuko grew up believing that if you were reasonably talented and invested sincere effort in the right areas, you would achieve success in your career, and economic rewards to match. The daughter of mainstream Japanese parents, who encouraged her to excel in school and work, Yasuko earned her degree at a first-class university (in a country where university rankings are discussed like vintages of Cabernet).

She went to work for one of the most famous financial institutions in the world. Still in her twenties, she already has compiled a long

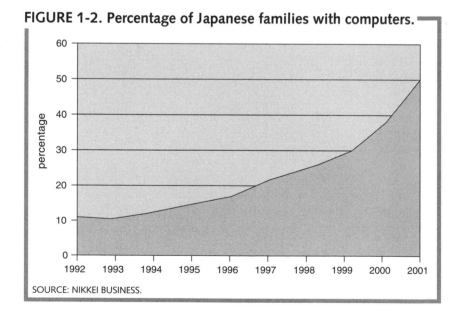

FIGURE 1-2. Percentage of Japanese families with computers.

SOURCE: NIKKEI BUSINESS.

record of working hard to achieve the right goals. And she has not shrunk from technology; she was an early adopter of the Internet, by Japanese standards, not to mention her i-mode phone. Yet Yasuko knows that, somehow, a lasting change is passing her by. She is modern, successful, and wired...yet not part of the new generation. And that generation, she fears, may be remaking Japan.

> *"Sure, I have an i-mode phone, but there are so many people who use it so much more than I do. I think you really need to find someone who was raised on these kinds of things. You know those young people who started using pagers when they were in junior high school."*

Did she mean drug dealers?

"No!" Yasuko sounds offended. "I mean that generation that was raised carrying around electronic devices. I wasn't."

Even though she's a young, computer-savvy professional, Yasuko isn't being modest when she claims not to have grown up with digital gadgets. Nor is she unusual. When she graduated from college in 1997 and took her first job, she had never touched a computer. In fact, electronics in general were more than a bit of a mystery to her. Yasuko was raised by parents who were, in her words, "old fashioned." They hadn't allowed video games in the home. They'd never considered using a mobile phone. Don't get us wrong; Yasuko's parents weren't Luddites. Nor had they blocked her from technology because she was a girl. To them, most electronic devices—especially consumer technology and new gadgets that did not directly fill some traditional, productive purpose—were irrelevant to success, or at least not very important. Certainly they weren't as valuable as another few hours of *juku*, Japanese cram school, or more time practicing the piano.

Her parents poured out their love by providing their firstborn daughter with all the encouragement, resources, habits, and attitudes that led to success...in the old world. The result? Yasuko presents an impressive veneer of the modern Japanese career woman, but beneath it her attitudes and beliefs, her model of how the world works, the way she thinks—all these predate the Information Revolution. Mama and Papa Sato lovingly, relentlessly instilled good old-fashioned *analog* values in their daughter.

Through her college years, Yasuko carried on the tradition with no deviation at all. So, compared to an American or European of the same age, Yasuko would have seemed, back then, electronically challenged. But she wasn't alone. In 1997, most of her peers in Japan, male and female, didn't have a clue about computers, the Internet, or electronic communication.

If You're Not Part of the Steamroller...

Five years later, they all do. Yasuko and her friends have been caught in the middle of a revolution. Granted, it has been a subtle one— almost invisible. Many things don't seem to have changed. The fundamentals, in fact, are completely the same: People still work and earn money; no one died on the barricades of this revolution; there haven't even been riots; government still goes on as it did before. And although some visible changes have taken place, they seem transient.

Millions of Japanese teens carry i-mode phones. But, then, aren't Japanese teens prone to fads and gadgets? Yes...but this is a case where small differences matter. The i-mode, and the class of devices that it represents (mobile, personal network connections) are not Walkmen. Ringtones are not Pokemon. This is powerful, many-to-many, interactive communications technology that's with you all the time. Even when new users are focused on some seemingly trivial purpose, like changing ringtones, they are learning how to use the technology. And once that barrier is broken, more important applications always seem to follow.

Yasuko senses the difference. Even though she might classify herself a casualty of this revolution, and certainly not a leader, she knows that these devices, which give people the ability to communicate, using voice or data, any time and any place, change everything. The changes seem small at first—in her case, they certainly did. But once set into motion, they work their way into important, almost invisible processes. Long-established patterns begin to shift; barriers and guidelines erode. Over time, the economic landscape is transformed. And one company has been instrumental in enabling Japan to lead this transformation: NTT DoCoMo.

FIGURE 1-3. Percentage of Japanese who use the Internet, by year.

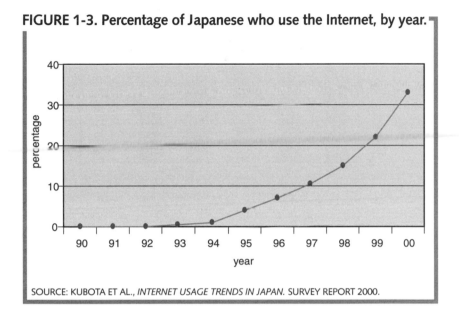

SOURCE: KUBOTA ET AL., *INTERNET USAGE TRENDS IN JAPAN*. SURVEY REPORT 2000.

Blame It on the Boyfriend

Yasuko was first introduced to NTT DoCoMo in 1998. About a year and a half into her first job, she reluctantly decided to buy a mobile phone. She had always avoided them for aesthetic reasons as well as practical ones. She thought that the people using cell phones in public places were rude louts. She hated the loud rings. She could not figure out why these people liked to disturb others, let alone sacrifice the privacy of their own conversations. But Yasuko was in love. And her boyfriend wanted to be able to get in touch with her outside the short windows of her evenings at home—they could make spontaneous plans to meet after work, for instance.

So Yasuko relented. She figured there was really no harm in carrying the device. It was, after all, small enough to disappear into a handbag. And she had a plan. She would only give out her number to her

FIGURE 1-4. Percentage of Japanese using the Internet, by age.

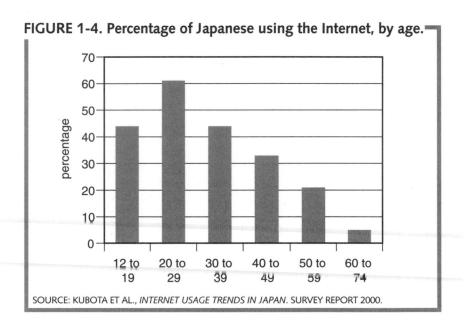

SOURCE: KUBOTA ET AL., *INTERNET USAGE TRENDS IN JAPAN*. SURVEY REPORT 2000.

FIGURE 1-5. Japanese experience with the Internet: November 2000.

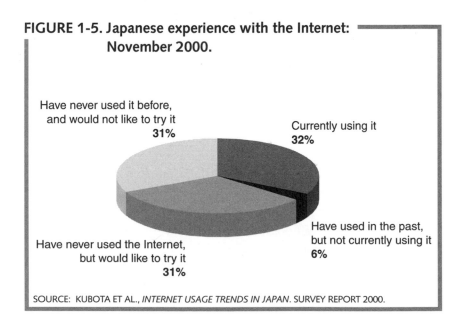

SOURCE: KUBOTA ET AL., *INTERNET USAGE TRENDS IN JAPAN*. SURVEY REPORT 2000.

boyfriend, her mother, and a few personal friends who she knew wouldn't disturb her at work or in the middle of the night. She would always keep it off when she was around other people. Yasuko was going to control when and where she used this thing.

At the time, Japan had lots of mobile phone service providers. And there were many different phones on the market. As in the United States and Europe, the phones' features, underlying network capabilities, and price structure varied widely and changed all the time. But Yasuko was not interested in becoming an expert on mobile phones or rate plans. That seemed boring. So she asked her boyfriend which phone she should purchase and which service made the most sense. He suggested DoCoMo's Citiphone.

Nippon Telephone and Telegraph, DoCoMo's parent company, is the Ma Bell of Japan. Even its acronym is suggestive. For a reluctant user like Yasuko, what would be less threatening than good old NTT? The Citiphone service also had the advantage of being relatively inexpensive for high-volume users. Here, too, love entered in; Yasuko's boyfriend planned on talking *a lot*.

FIGURE 1-6. Cell phone companies in Japan: 1998 subscribers.

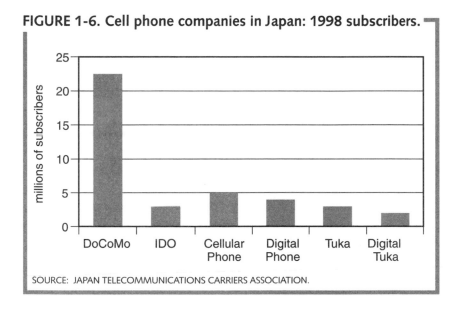

SOURCE: JAPAN TELECOMMUNICATIONS CARRIERS ASSOCIATION.

Creeping Cellularitis

At first, Yasuko's phone spent a lot of time "sleeping" in her handbag. As she had predicted, she could not see any good reason or opportunity to use it. If she had anything really important to say, she preferred to get home and say it on a regular phone. Yasuko did have a significant commute: She worked in Yokohama and was living with her family a full hour away. But talking on mobile phones is prohibited on Japanese trains (see Figure 1-7) and on even-numbered cars on the Tokyu line in Tokyo, for instance, the phone is supposed to be turned off completely (see Figure 1-8). And Yasuko certainly wasn't going to use the gadget to disrupt work. It just always seemed to her that there was no phone call so important that she couldn't wait a few minutes to get to a "normal" phone.

FIGURE 1-7. No talking.

Then, she began to understand the wonders of mobility.

Ah, Sweet Mystery of Life

> *"Finally, though, I began making occasional calls with my cell phone. After I started using it, I found it was pretty convenient."*

Though she doesn't come right out and say so, Yasuko finally began to try this new technology, because of love (romantic and parental)...that and the construction techniques in Japanese homes. Even after a decade of recession, the Japanese are affluent by any

FIGURE 1-8. Phones turned off.

電源をお切りください
Please switch off
the cellular phone.

2号車

standard. But, famously, their houses are smaller than those of Americans and Europeans. And the walls are literally paper thin. Of course, the Japanese norm is to provide privacy through behavior, not space. (When he first moved to Japan, it took John weeks to accept that when Japanese neighbors aren't supposed to hear you they insist, even believe, that they literally do not hear. To a curious American, this seems like an amazing act of will, right up there with firewalking.) Still, privacy poses a challenge for any young person.

Once Yasuko became a teenager, even simple chats with her girlfriends had begun to call for nuanced language or hushed whispers. Not that the dutiful Yasuko really wanted to have any shocking conversations. But, as she says, "You know, you don't want your parents to know everything about your life." Back then, if she really wanted to say something important, she'd grab her umbrella and walk down the street, wait for a pay phone to free up, and *still* usually have to talk quietly because someone else was often in line behind her waiting to use the phone, and thus could hear the entire exchange. But once she began using her mobile phone she found she could say all of those things on her walk home from the train station—or at night she could settle in at the little neighborhood coffee shop and chat on the phone in relative anonymity and comfort. The mobility of the device let her duck outside for particularly sensitive exchanges.

Sato's sixteen-year-old dog, Jerry, also probably owes a few of those years to cellular technology. Yasuko had always believed it was important to take the dog for a short walk, but once she accepted wireless as a real phone, the walks grew a little longer. If she talked while she walked, she could even discuss the most private of subjects;

no one was likely to hear enough of any particular conversation to really make a difference. So whenever Yasuko found herself deep in a conversation and not yet ready to go home, Jerry's constitutionals became marathons.

One third of the housing in Tokyo averages only

121 square feet, while the average Japanese home is

650 square feet. Even outside Tokyo, the average home

for a family of three is still under 1,000 square feet.

Only for the Phone-Literate

In February 1999, NTT DoCoMo came to market with an entirely new product: the i-mode phone. In addition to the voice capabilities that Yasuko had grown used to, the new phone allowed for Internet connectivity. These new capabilities excited technophiles but held little interest for her. That wasn't because she was uninterested in the Internet. Quite the contrary; in her first few years on the job, Yasuko had unexpectedly grown to love the power of computers.

Her company was a traditional Japanese firm. "It was not at all like the U.S. style where everyone has a computer on their desk at work." In Yasuko's workgroup, one computer terminal served five employees. (And this was in the finance/accounting section!) The shared computer sat near a window. As a member of the section, you could get up from your workstation and go to the computer to gather information. But if you did, you would be away from your phone and therefore out of touch with other company members and the outside world—a real sacrifice by Western standards, but far worse in consensus-driven Japan. There was another problem, too: At that time, using a computer directly was thought of as pretty menial work. So when Yasuko joined the group as a young and inexperienced female, it was not surprising that her superiors decided that she should log the bulk of the computer time.

Yasuko had graduated from Waseda University, one of the top schools in Japan, but her degree was in Asian history—not a major that requires a huge amount of computer expertise. The first day that she had to deal with the computer, a young man from the information technology department showed up and explained how to turn on the unfamiliar device. Yasuko learned quickly, though, at least in those areas where the system had clear, practical value. (She had heard a lot about the Internet, for instance, but connections were not possible from her work computer, and she wasn't really sure what she'd use the Internet for anyway.)

Soon she was actually teaching others how to use the proprietary accounting packages on the old Hitachi workstation. Before long, she could no longer be considered a bit player in her section. A year or so later, with her growing confidence in the use of computers, Yasuko took a huge leap: She got her own laptop computer. With that, she became a part of the e-mail generation and found that it was even really useful in her work. Now, in retrospect, she admits that she could "never go back to those pre-Internet days." Yasuko has never had any affection for high-tech devices themselves, but she has always *loved* the freedom, reach, and responsiveness the devices put within her grasp.

As computer use was changing Yasuko, it also changed traditional Japanese attitudes. The value of information processing became obvious to more and more managers. So over time, computer skills began to be respected, computer users began to win status, and the business capabilities that computers made possible began to be taken for granted. Indeed, computers (and the related communications technologies) moved from menial status to a favored topic of conversation among many rising employees, "particularly the men." According to Yasuko, these guys literally love technology: "they are always talking about gadgets—gigabits and megabytes—that kinda stuff."

FIGURE 1-9. Purpose of mobile phone usage in Japan.

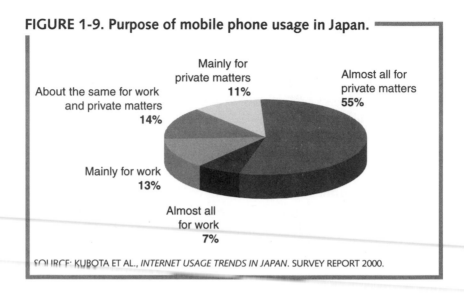

SOURCE: KUBOTA ET AL., *INTERNET USAGE TRENDS IN JAPAN*. SURVEY REPORT 2000.

FIGURE 1-10. Primary form of access to the Internet in Japan: December 2000.

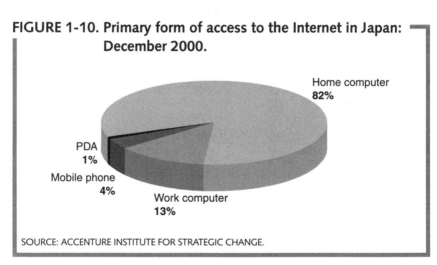

SOURCE: ACCENTURE INSTITUTE FOR STRATEGIC CHANGE.

Yasuko admits it might be good for her career to take part in such conversations, but she just can't bring herself to care about technology itself. It doesn't seem serious enough. She's happy to adopt technology when it clearly will help her, but *only* then. Perhaps because of her upbringing, she doesn't have the genuine feelings she would need to join the tech lovers. But, feelings aside, it's clear that those who do chat gigabits are not only indulging a genuine passion but also building strong personal relationships—and establishing credibility with one another as fellow members of the rising digital elite. As they move up through the ranks together, they'll remember who among them is advanced, technologically savvy, ready for innovation.

An April 2001 study by Japan's Ministry of

Public Management reported that 34.5 million

subscribers access the Internet through their cellular

service—almost matching the 37.2 million people

accessing it through fixed-line connections.

Masako Loves I-mode

Yasuko insists that, when it comes to mobile technology, she is the wrong Sato. "You should really be talking to my sister about this. It is Masako's generation that is really using i-mode." Masako is attending nursing school in Tokyo and living at home. She has not achieved the career and academic success that Yasuko has. But when it comes to i-mode, she is a star; she does all the things that a good i-mode generation person would be expected to do.

Masako Goes Mobile—Always

Masako uses her mobile phone a lot. Even though she's a student, she racks up at least $150 a month in mobile phone charges. "When she goes over $200 in a single month, my mother really gets upset," says Yasuko.

Masako Accessorizes

Any good mobile phone user in Japan—whether they use DoCoMo, J-Phone, or Au—knows about carrying straps. Yasuko has one, with kyoro-chan on it. (Kyoro is a retro *anime* character, an old cartoon that "is old enough to be cute again.") Masako, on the other hand, has a whole wardrobe of them.

Masako Hacks

Japanese users also know the importance of ringtones (*chakumelo*) and screensavers. Yasuko uses a screensaver on her PC but never bothered to download one for her phone. She does use different ringtones for different functions (e.g., calls where caller ID isn't known sound distinctive). For Masako, though, downloading *chakumelo* from a free site is something of a hobby; she installs a new one every couple of weeks.

Box 1-1. Ringtones.

If you don't understand what a ringtone is, you are probably American. It seems like everyone else in the world has embraced the use of personalized ringtones. John is too embarrassed to have his phone go off in a meeting, so he usually keeps it on vibrate. But one of the most conservative, staid academics John knows—a German—doesn't seem to have any qualms at all about the theme to *Mission Impossible* bursting forth from his briefcase all day long. It rang during a business meeting one day. The room erupted with laughter when they saw him going for his bag; the contrast with Tom Cruise was just too striking.

Masako Does Data

Finally, Masako does data on her phone—all the time. (Yasuko doesn't. Even her Citiphone service allowed her to send short mails, but she never used it.) From looking up train schedules, to making reservations at restaurants, to buying movie tickets, Masako does everything on the train as she commutes to and from school, or as she sits in a pub with her friends. And, naturally, this is her favorite mode for e-mails. The level of involvement this provides—nearly constant interaction with her friends and colleagues, the ability to be an active, visible part of discussions that go on with almost no regard for boundaries of the work day—is a huge competitive advantage in most careers. It's an expansion, really, of the bonding Yasuko sees among her gadget-loving (primarily male) colleagues.

Torn Between Two Lovers

As she says, Yasuko is an i-mode user, too, but a very different one. It all started when she returned from a year in school in the United States. She found she really needed a phone again; in the nine short months she was out of the country, cell phones had moved from a convenience to an absolute requirement. Once again, she consulted a technophile—this time not her boyfriend but rather Masako, who said the cheapest place to buy a phone was not one of the big discount stores, but a small shop on an almost forgotten street in Yokohama—a real hole in the wall.

Yasuko read a lot about phones before she made her decision. (The only serious competitor to i-mode was J-Phone's camera phone, which debuted to a lot of hype. But in the end, Yasuko went with the numbers. Even in the summer of 2001, she saw competition possibly heating up for NTT DoCoMo but would not have bet on any other company.)

Even though her new phone is much more capable than her old one, Yasuko still uses it in much the same way. As before, only a few friends have her number; not even her boss does (though he does have her home number). She still uses voice more heavily than she expected before going mobile. But she hardly uses the "i" functions of her phone at all. (And she is not alone; it's a standing joke among some of her friends that the "i" button on the phones is there to collect dust.) Yasuko loves the mobility of i-mode, but only for voice. She also loves e-mail. She just can't seem to bring those two passions together to embrace a single device the way Masako and some of the boys in the office have. Because she first met the Internet on the PC, Yasuko says she'll never want to use a phone as her main way to access it. "Those who start with the Internet on the phone get used to it, and they don't seem to mind the small screens and the limited keypad," she says.

Box 1-2. How mobile services are changing the "little" things.

Everyone wants to be part of history. If history includes the details of everyday life, then many of us will soon get that wish. Comments from hundreds of mobile users worldwide suggest that things we've taken for granted our whole lives will soon be changing. For instance:

Sayonara, Seiko

The invention of a mechanical clock dates back to the thirteenth or early fourteenth century. For our entire adult lives, the wristwatch has been an extension of our bodies. Do you know a single person who doesn't wear one? But to our surprise, many in Japan no longer wear watches at all; instead, they use their mobile phones. High school students are even allowed to keep wireless devices on their desks, just to keep track of time.

Watches may continue as jewelry, but for keeping time—and for keeping us on time—wireless devices are far more powerful. They are automatically synchronized by the service provider, increasingly include schedule functions, and let communications replace rigid scheduling. The concept of meeting someone at an exact time is fast disappearing. Instead, many users just call or message a friend on wireless, see where they are currently, and set a meeting place on the fly.

Ta Ta, *Time* Magazine

In countries where cell phones are abundant, magazines, books, newspapers, and other printed publications are being replaced. A thirty-five-year-old male professional in Japan put it this way: "I no longer need to spend money on magazines or newspapers; I can get all of this information from the Internet." His mobile device is easy to carry on a train and accessible at the airport while he's waiting for a flight to take off. "The time I used to spend reading books I now spend playing on my cell phone," said another Japanese respondent. "I don't know if it's good or bad."

Farewell, Film and Faxes

Digital cameras already let you see and edit your photographs right away; fast, instant transmission via wireless is now making it easy to share them with just about anyone. In an economy where this is routine, film, prints, and faxes become truly obsolete—and a whole new way of working becomes the norm. "I use my [i-mode phone] for sending important digital photo images to clients. It has made my job so much more efficient. The client no longer has to come on site to view a potential problem," said a Japanese professional working in the construction industry. In theory, his U.S. counterpart could do that today. But since he can't send the digital file on wireless, he's stuck with returning to the office and hooking up to a desktop computer first. This is better than buying film, waiting for a print, and using FedEx—but it's slow and inconvenient enough that in many cases he just won't bother.

Ciao, Currency

In Norway and Finland, you can buy soda from machines by pushing a button on your cell phone. In some cases, that's the only way to buy. Singapore's government has announced plans to discontinue printing notes and minting coins by the year 2008. And other mobile paper equivalents are headed the same way: In Japan, if you want a discount on your Wendy's hamburger, you just download a "coupon"—a single color screen—on your cell phone and show it at the counter. After centuries of relying on printed paper to represent value, the leaders in the wireless economy seem to be ushering in a new era.

Goodbye, Grammar

Language rules and sentence structure are now out the window. Senior executives in the U.K. noticed a dramatic change in communication styles, particularly in letter writing etiquette. These folks complained that very few people write proper letters in today's electronic world. People simply jot down a couple of lines in a fax or e-mail, frequently ignoring standard salutations, punctuation, and grammar. Short text messages routinely ignore capital letters and even spelling: "U" instead of "you" becomes quite normal. Many perceive these changes as "rude," but they are increasingly common. And like many generational changes, they soon become invisible.

Passion Is Destiny

These are times of rapid change for everyone. In just a few years, Yasuko has gone from computer novice, to local expert, to a solid participant in an increasingly wireless world. She's not at the leading edge. "You can see how analog I still am," she says, pointing out that the guys at work are often real mobile data lovers. One mid-thirties ("and highly paid") manager at work reads the newspaper sites on the train every morning. Yasuko, by contrast, doesn't need to do that; she always takes the actual newspaper on the train with her to work—or reads it over coffee first thing in the morning. That seems perfectly sensible. So why does she feel uncomfortable about it?

Meanwhile, technology keeps raising the bar—and, perhaps, if it is successful, exciting new passions. In October 2001, NTT DoCoMo officially launched its third generation (3G) high-speed wireless Internet service in Tokyo. For Yasuko, is the world's first instance of 3G a new opportunity to leap ahead in her career or simply another gadget? At this point, she's not sure. She is not sure she needs all that speed right now. But she does plan to move into a new apartment soon and when she does, she doesn't want to have to pay for a wired phone line. "The problem is what to do about my Internet connection for my laptop?"

Yasuko believes that if the new service can function as an "intermediary without the cord" to her computer, then she'll sign up immediately. She envisions a day when she could carry a small, very thin keyboard with her as well; this would enable her to input personal e-mail during the day without using her work computer for personal correspondence. As Yasuko describes the value of that connectivity, you can hear the passion and longing in her voice. "I'd never be out of touch with any part of my life…"

For an active, ambitious, professional, it's a natural. Yasuko clearly has the right idea. The question is, will her love of technology's *results* drive her to follow through? And what will Masako (who loves the i-mode's fashion value) and the guys in the office (who just love gadgets) be doing in the meantime?

Why Yasuko Matters

What do all these excitable i-mode users have to teach the rest of us? What does Yasuko's story hold for *your* business? Simple: the key to that attention problem we all confront. (You *remember*...how to get your innovation—the one your company's future may depend on—noticed, tried, embraced, even loved.)

Yasuko, Masako, and the tech-boys back at the office—these and millions more just like them—are the people who gave DoCoMo success. Without their adopting i-mode (seemingly random decisions, made sometimes for reasons they didn't understand, using assumptions that proved to be wrong), none of us, on this side of the Pacific, would have heard about i-mode. How did DoCoMo capture their attention, money, and passion? How can we do the same? By inspiring the right kind of love affair.

Ring Mah Bell?

The traditional approach begins with a bell curve that segments your market into who is likely to adopt a new technology when.

The idea is that different customers tend to dive into innovative approaches early or late. In some cases, it almost doesn't matter what those innovations are. This is a handy framework, and a useful way to begin thinking about who needs to know about, try, and use your product. Yasuko, for example, falls into the early majority. Though circumstances—such as her boyfriend or her initial computer assignment—may nudge her to adopt a new technology fairly early in its life, she is attracted strictly by what the technology can do for her. The tech-boys at her office, on the other hand, are standard early adopters.

Somewhere in their orbit, maybe even in their group, will be an innnovator—the kind of person who found out about i-mode first and tried it early, when there were few other users to learn from, less return on the investment, and more adoption hassles. These are the famous pioneers, complete with the arrows in their backs. And they wouldn't have it any other way. Masako is an early adopter, too, but with a twist; the innovators she learns from focus more on fashion than on technology.

Elsewhere on i-mode's subscriber list are millions of late adopters—customers more conservative than Yasuko, who waited until i-mode was proven and of obvious practical value, before jumping in. Finally, there are the laggards, who may not get i-mode for years, if ever.

FIGURE 1-11. Corn-fed innovation.

The standard technology adoption curve, seen on PowerPoint slides all over the world, dates back to at least as far as the 1930s, when Bruce Ryan and Neal Gross studied the way farmers adopted hybrid seed corn, and to Everett Rogers's *Diffusion of Innovations*, first published in 1962. The corn innovation was clearly superior to the alternatives, so much so that, eventually, all farmers in the area they studied switched over. But, even though they faced similar incentives, the farmers didn't all adopt it at once. In detailing that, Ryan and Gross divided them into groups that look like this:

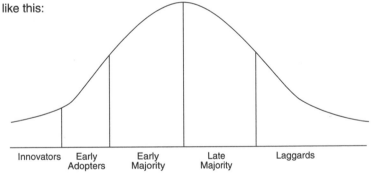

| Innovators | Early Adopters | Early Majority | Late Majority | Laggards |

This traditional curve includes five categories: innovators, early adopters, early majority, late majority, and laggards.

In recent years, this traditional approach has been modified by a really useful observation: Each of these groups adopts technology, or any innovation, for different reasons. And, if you're trying to generate adoption for your product, that can create challenges. That's only one of the problems you face as your sales move from innovators to the increasingly conservative groups, where you can make real money.[2]

Box 1-3. A man without love?

One of John's most vivid childhood memories has his eighty-year-old Mormon grandmother dressed in a purple bell-bottom pantsuit…getting ready for an Englebert Humperdinck concert. It's a reminder—impossible to forget, really—of why the niche populations, like fashion trendsetters and geeks, are so important.

All of us with an innovation (a product, a business, an ad campaign) hope, at some level, that our products will be wildly, inexplicably POPULAR. The most popular products and services don't always win critical praise, but everyone uses them. What more could you want?

So all of us hope to accomplish what Engelbert did. Somehow, his passionate yet flower-powered message made it not only all the way to Utah, but all the way to Grandma. Now mind you, Grandma wasn't rabid. She didn't try to convert everyone she met to the religion of Humperdinck, but she did buy: the concert tickets, the pantsuit, the albums. In other words, like millions of others who were supposed to be left out of this new and fashionable trend, she bought into pop culture.

Of course, in the four years it took between Woodstock and Grandma's epiphany, the cult of Humperdinck undoubtedly passed through several groups. There were the brave young souls who invested their social capital in buying his records when no one had heard of him. There were those kids' (far more numerous) peers, who added their capital by following along, receiving of course a lower but more secure rate of return. There were the trendy parents who caught the bug. And somewhere, maybe a group or two later, there was Grandma. The Engelbert industry would have made far less money for its investors if Grandma and her friends hadn't been caught up; but they would never have made a dollar if they hadn't first caught the ear of the ruthless trendsetters who, by Grandma's day, were denying they'd even heard of Humperdinck.

DoCoMo's i-mode became a hit partly because it appealed to two completely separate groups of innovators: fashion-conscious young people, like Masako or her cutting-edge role models, and traditional geeks who fed the early-adopter guys in Yasuko's office. As we have seen, any hit starts with a few real believers. In fashion circles, these can be those in "high society"—wealthy enough to buy the designer styles they see on a runway in Milan or Paris. Or they could be the young hipsters in Tribeca who could never afford high-end fashion but who experiment with less expensive combinations of clothing, shoes, and headgear. To someone firmly in the mainstream, the hipsters can be invisible, even frumpy looking. But for the Yasukos of the fashion market, they set the direction. Either hipsters or the high end can start a fad, but they have to love the product so much they can talk about little else—at least for a few days.

In technology circles the fashion mavens are often "geeks"—the guys (and we use this term advisedly) who cruise the aisles of Fry's Electronics looking for the latest gizmo to use with their thing-a-majig. They, at the very least, play around with every new product out there. Although this innovator population can prove invaluable, it can also be a vicious, double-edged sword. The things they buy, use, and like become social capital at their cocktail-party equivalents—for them, it is better than passing along a great stock tip, or chatting up a wonderful new vacation hideaway. But the things they try and *don't* like—those are anathema. On the Internet, in coffee-break conversations, and on the phone they castigate the product. They seem intent on reducing the inventor, the financial backers, and even the product itself to a weeping heap through their nasty, caustic comments. It becomes a holy cause to make sure the product never gets a toehold. It's a war they can win, too.

"Early adopters are a scary bunch. They love new

features, so they will request more bells and whistles

in your product....If you try to explain that you're trying

to keep your product simple and relevant for novices,

they intepret this as unresponsiveness or stupidity."

—GUY KAWASAKI

Remember DiVX? When DVD hadn't quite crossed over beyond the innovators (our geeks), electronics giant Phillips and retail power-house Circuit City collaborated to develop a format that reduced the price of buying a DVD to, essentially, the price of a video rental. The catch was that, if you wanted to watch it again, you had to pay again (on a sliding scale). It sounds like a great match for most consumers. But the techies hated it and—of course—badmouthed it incessantly. Whether the mass market would have liked the model or not, DiVX was quickly forgotten.

DoCoMo's home run was developing a product that appealed to both groups. You don't find that too often, but when you do...stand back. By getting the geeks and the fashionable to agree on a single product, the masses in the middle were assaulted on two different (and usually antagonistic) fronts. The result was pretty darn close to impossible to resist. General appeal was born. We should all hope to be so good (and perhaps so lucky).

Box 1-4. What's with this chasm?

In *Crossing the Chasm*, author Geoffrey Moore points out that the lines between the segments on the standard technology adoption curve aren't just for decoration or statistics; each of these groups wants different things. The difference between early adopters and the early majority is especially crucial. Moore analyzes a number of examples from the high-tech industry and concludes that while the customers in these two groups may look the same (same size company, same size order, etc.) and buy the same products, they are really purchasing very different things.

Early adopters are looking to your innovation to serve as a change agent; they want to do things differently. Buyers in the early majority are shopping for productivity improvement. They want you to help them do their accustomed tasks better. These early majority buyers can be lucrative, but before they buy they want the security of hearing from people like themselves that your innovation is valuable. Hearing from early adopters—who by definition are willing to invest more and take more risks—does not help them. Early adopter satisfaction doesn't necessarily translate into mass appeal. This creates the "chasm" into which your innovation might easily fall.

Getting Serious

The standard tools are great. But if bell-curve-and-chasm thinking can explain generations of techno winners, why are we talking about love stories? Because the world has changed. For the challenge that DoCoMo faced—which, unfortunately, is the same challenge most of us face now in launching new information products—the standard tools just aren't enough. Five big factors make technology adoption a whole new ball game:

■ *We're all overwhelmed by change.* Some of us love it, some of us hate it, but all of us face faster, more sustained innovation, on many more fronts, than our parents did. (Or even our older siblings—remember Yasuko and her sister?) More is changing faster, and we know about it sooner.

■ *Users are more important.* Classic tech-adoption studies tend to analyze B2B products, things that are simple to use, technologies where performance is objective. Many innovations that matter today are more like consumer products. Even if intended for a business audience, the user's individual and unpredictable preferences matter—a lot.

■ *Information products are different.* The innovations we offer are often information products—some mix of device, service, and information, all bundled together with a usage pattern and a business model that both buyer and seller have to think through. That's very different from a faster hard disk, a longer-lasting tire, or more robust seed corn. So it's harder to know what you want; harder to know what a fair price would be; harder to know if the thing is even working right. All that adds risk and inconvenience—thus subtracting possible customers.

■ *Products are getting personal.* Because user preference matters so much, techy products are getting very personal. That makes technology adoption more like the fashion industry—very hits-driven, very hard to predict. Who can tell, before the customers start buying, whether Palms or iPaqs will dominate?

■ *Innovation now means new product TYPES.* Many innovations now have no real predecessor. Starbucks sells coffee, but what it really sells is an experience that, for 90 percent of the U.S. market, simply hadn't been imagined before. TiVo seems comparable to a VCR but really offers an entirely different kind of value. In cases like these, customers must guess what they want in this product, or if they want it at all. The innovator—and remember, we are all either innovating or heading to the scrap heap—has a much tougher job.

Inside the Bell Curve

All five barriers certainly applied to i-mode. Yet DoCoMo somehow vaulted over all of them. That's the love factor. In our view, i-mode operated way beyond the level of bell curves and market segmentation. The adoption battle was won at a much deeper psychological level, capturing the emotions of customers alone and in groups. Fundamentally, DoCoMo created a true hit product by inspiring passion—this really is a love story—in the right groups of people.

Research to support this comes from two scientific hot spots that *seem* far removed from business: the emerging, highly quantitative science of complexity, and the psychology behind social epidemics (everything from teen smoking to fashion trends).

Making Hits Happen

The computer modelers and quant jocks who study complexity point out that a lot of interesting systems, such as the earth's climate, are so complex that they simply cannot be modeled as simple, linear machines. The would-be modeler is facing too much uncertainty, and too many nonlinear events. One scientist has said that systems like these function "on the edge of chaos and order." That is, they're not predictable—put that spreadsheet model away. But they're not truly random, either. We can begin to anticipate how they act, but only by observing their behavior over time and working to identify the principles and patterns that tend to emerge. One such pattern is the tendency toward increasing returns—something we've all noticed in today's attention-poor economy, where the brand, Web site, or product that is ahead tends to pull farther ahead. To these scientists, any hits-driven business (and that includes much of the innovation we care about) is a complex system.

One such expert who has used the tools of complexity to analyze business problems, Winslow Farrell, points out that "Hits emerge as a function of the conversation started around a product or idea." He goes on to recommend that if you want to make your product a hit, you "look at how people relate to products, and to each other through them."[3] In other words, in shaping hits, interpersonal relationships are critical. This, we believe, becomes dramatically more important when the technology itself literally involves communication among people—like i-mode, which changed how Yasuko related to her bosses (she became more tech savvy), to her parents (more independent), and her boyfriend (closer, faster, and yet ultimately more independent).

Tipping

A completely different take on how particular people, and their passions, drive technology adoption comes from the social dynamics that author Malcolm Gladwell labeled "tipping points." A wide range of studies, on many topics, shows that if you want to create a "behavioral epidemic," then the right people are central. (The market and the product matter too, of course.) Consider a hit that, unfortunately, is even more dramatic than i-mode: teen smoking. Despite years of antismoking ad campaigns, parental efforts, laws, school regulations, and education, teens have continued to take up smoking, often in increasing numbers. Gladwell's analysis concludes that it's all about the *kinds* of people who start the smoking in each new group of teens—the innovators on that particular technology adoption curve. He explains that the very individuals most likely to visibly try smoking first are those independent, risk-taking teens who have enormous influence over their peers. As he says, "Smoking was never cool. *Smokers* are cool....a select few are responsible for driving the epidemic forward."[4]

In adopting a new product, people of all ages look to their peers. And some peers matter much more than others. A student of complexity might add, although you can't always predict ahead of time which peers will have the most influence, you can identify them on the fly—if you're quick.

From either point of view, complex phenomenon or social epidemic, if what you need is a successful innovation, then you're in the business of creating hits. DoCoMo is, and it certainly has! Some would argue that a "real" high technology product, with hard differences in performance and cost—and i-mode could be included—can't be analyzed like a hit record or a clothing fad. At least for consumer products, we disagree. Yes, consumers care about features, functions, and costs. But in an environment where even the most naive customer knows that cost is constantly dropping, and functionality constantly increasing, do those factors really drive decisions?

In the case of i-mode, how did millions of young Japanese decide that now was the time they *needed* a data-capable mobile phone? Or Bandai screensavers? And, again, the science from both perspectives tells us that to make your innovation a hit, you have to focus on the right people, as people—just as DoCoMo did. The kind of personal gravitation that pulled both Yasuko and Masako into i-mode's orbit is crucial. Human passion, love, is what it took to capture their attention and use. And without that, without the first wave of early adopters, i-mode would have failed completely.

What the World Needs Now

So, innovation is imperative, adoption is the hard part, the key to adoption is people, and—for i-mode—love was a big part of getting those crucial first people. Even if "love is the answer," what are we supposed to do about all that? How can we use love to make our own products runaway hits like i-mode? Begin with four principles:

1. *Promote personal passions.* If looking at i-mode users—especially at the crucial first waves that started it all—tells us anything, it's that the seemingly small things that individual people care about (keeping in touch with boyfriends, impulsively having private chats,

impressing friends with a powerful gadget or a new fashion accessory) can drive product adoption. (Our research has seen similar patterns in wireless data's other great hot spot, Northern Europe, where user passion for keeping in touch with other people has created adoption rates much higher than we see in the United States.) And the research in cognitive psychology shows why. A number of studies have shown that we humans are much better at processing complex information if it has to do with other humans, rather than with abstractions—including the analytic concepts like market share or service quality that we all work with every day.

"Starting epidemics requires concentrating resources

on a few key areas. Connectors, Mavens, and Salesmen

are responsible for starting word-of-mouth epidemics,

which means...your resources ought to be solely

concentrated on those three groups. No one else matters."

—MALCOLM GLADWELL

There's a powerful evolutionary reason: As social animals, our species has survived over millennia by paying special attention to other humans and sentient creatures—a tendency that we suspect kicks in strongly at times of stress and overload. Most important, there's a strong human theme apparent in the customers who made i-mode a runaway success. Think of Yasuko, Masako, and the boys in the office. They were different types of crucial early customers, but all of them bought i-mode because they were responding to *people*: bosses, boyfriends, pals at the office. So, if there is any chance at all, look for ways that your innovation can be important to users on a human level. *Especially watch for ways that adopting your product can bring them closer to each other, gain them status, or make them feel good socially.*

Box 1-5. Rolling the DICE-E.

Guy Kawasaki, who cut his teeth on the explosive adoption of the original Macintosh, lists five attributes (which he abbreviates DICE-E) for great products.[5] Every one is about how customers feel. Kawasaki argues that great products are:

1. **Deep.** The desires that these products satisfied were so deep that you didn't even know you had them before you bought.
2. **Indulging.** The product is more than you really need and costs more than you really needed to pay.
3. **Complete.** Great documentation, service, and support make this feel complete.
4. **Elegant.** Great elegant design makes complex, new products easy and even fun to use.
5. **Evocative.** The product evokes an emotional response (hopefully a good one).

---

2. *Go beyond the mainstream.* At least for consumer information products—and what product today isn't?—go beyond what seem like rational economic reasons for customers to buy. Look at the original product evangelist, Guy Kawasaki. With Macintosh, Internet, and early-stage investor experience, he's been through the mill of getting new products adopted. And his five tests for defining great products,

as he naturally expresses them—see "Rolling the DICE-E"—are all about how customers *feel*.

The i-mode story teaches the same lesson: to get attention in a hyper-crowded environment, to vault over the many barriers to adoption, and finally to harness the social process that creates hits, your product has to grab customers beneath the sensible surface level of value propositions. Like Yasuko, they'll research and shop with their rational minds, but they'll *buy* and *use* and *recommend* for reasons they probably won't say out loud and may not understand. As with i-mode, those reasons can eventually flow through the entire market. How many mobile phones, purchased for emergency or business use, are actually valued for their ability to keep us connected with the people we care about even though we move around each day? Your job is to watch carefully whom your product appeals to, what they're using it for. *Don't depend on what customers say, especially in answering structured questions; watch what they are doing, and understand why.* Those unspoken forces are the energy that creates a hit product like i-mode.

3. Look for entry populations—and move fast when you find them. Those human needs are easiest to spot, at first, in fringe populations whose needs or desires place them ahead of more mainstream users. And, always, if your goal is to start a "social epidemic" around your product, it is small groups of people who hold that power. Bottom line? For both attracting first users and creating a wave of adoption that follows them, small and highly specific groups are crucial. These entry populations can move you into the mainstream, fast.

In DoCoMo's case, their original target audience was business buyers. That made analytic sense; these customers have money, are mobile, and seriously need key data. The value proposition made for some nice spreadsheets. So these were the targets, and initial i-mode content was heavily weighted toward the sites they would presumably want: travel, stocks, and so forth. But within two months, DoCoMo found that the most heavily frequented sites were the places to download great new ringtones and wallpaper. These were the things that techies, teens, and trendsetters—the people who actually saw i-mode's value first—wanted. And DoCoMo was incredibly astute in leveraging from these populations to reach, ultimately, not only the business customers they had first thought of, but millions more, as well. *So cater to and watch the people who value your product—even if they don't seem like a viable market by themselves.*

"Tucked in some recess at the back of our

minds is a wishful view of the

business world as predictable, plannable,

and controllable by our actions."

—W. BRIAN ARTHUR

---

4. *Plan to change your product.* When you think seriously about the challenge any new product faces, and the process by which i-mode became a hit, you come to know that planning and control are really impossible. That realization will make you (like the complexity scientists we have worked with) a huge fan of adaptive behavior. And you'll be in good company. Scientists and historians will tell you that adaptation has a long and honorable history. In fact, adaptation essentially *is* history. We're t-t-talkin 'bout evolution here—not a planned or predictable process, but one that proves incredibly powerful. A great deal of its power comes exactly because there is no one driving; the process just relentlessly searches for advantage, *even in places where no one expects it*, and adapts to use that advantage, as with the heat-regulating structures that, Stephen Jay Gould argues, eventually became wings.

You'd expect the guy who ran Citibank to be a fan of planning and control. Maybe. But Walter Wriston also noted that "the modern world financial system really evolved, as the unplanned result of communication satellites and engineers' control of the electromagnetic spectrum."[6] Leaders in robotics and AI have often demonstrated the power of rapid, simple adaptation versus heavy strategic planning in search of the optimum approach. And looking beyond business, Malcolm Gladwell concludes that, "Those who are successful at creating social epidemics do not just do what they think is right. They deliberately test their intuitions." By testing their intuitions and changing quickly when reality proved different, the folks at DoCoMo turned i-mode into the only full-fledged success in wireless Internet adoption. *So experiment boldly—look closely and deeply at what the experiment is telling you about users—and move fast to reconfigure your market, product, or business model into the hit it can become.*

Judging from DoCoMo's experience, that's exactly what it takes to "feel the love."

Notes

1. Thomas H. Davenport and John C. Beck, *The Attention Economy* (Boston: Harvard Business School Press, 2001).

2. Geoffrey A. Moore, *Crossing the Chasm* (New York: HarperBusiness, 1991).

3. Winslow Farrell, *How Hits Happen* (New York: HarperBusiness, 2000).

4. Malcolm Gladwell, *The Tipping Point: How Little Things Can Make a Big Difference* (Boston: Little Brown, 2000).

5. Guy Kawasaki, *Rules for Revolutionaries* (New York: HarperBusiness, 1999).

6. Richard Foster, *Innovation: The Attacker's Advantage* (New York: Summit, 1986).

CHAPTER TWO

Inequality

"Inequality...the measure of the
progress of the world."

—FELIX E. SCHELLING

THE DAY THE WAR ENDED, Keiji Tachikawa was six years old.
Like any six-year-old boy, he saw the world differently from how
adults see it. By our grown-up standards, he missed a lot. But he saw
enough. Even in the farm country where his family lived (Gifu prefecture, a light-year's difference from the frenzy of nearby Tokyo), Keiji
saw starvation, bitterness, and tears.

This suffering did not simply end when the war ended in 1945.
The occupying American army imposed great change on Japan—
change intended not only to protect the rest of the world from future
aggression, but also, sincerely, to improve the lot of the Japanese people. So the traditional empire not only had to rebuild its economy from
scratch, it also had to become a constitutional democracy. The United
States provided enormous help, but it also set the rules. One of those
rules was property reform. For the "landed class" Tachikawa clan, this
was yet another blow; when he was eight, young Keiji's family lost its
ancestral home.

* * * * *

Half a century later, Keiji Tachikawa has come far from that life in Gifu. Here at the beginning of the twenty-first century, he literally looks down on the Imperial Palace. His office is high inside one of the most modern buildings in Tokyo—a skyscraper so large that each elevator holds sixty-three people. Sixty-three! In just one elevator! And there are six elevators! You could put an ordinary Internet company, a whole dot-com, in each car and send the whole staff of hip young innovators all the way up to the twenty-seventh floor, to DoCoMo's lobby. If the child crusaders of the new economy were allowed to go further, many floors further, they could reach Keiji Tachikawa's office: the place where, as CEO, he makes daily decisions to support the vision of chairman Ohboshi and the growth that this vision has created—Japan's biggest success story in more than a decade. If they were allowed that far up, perhaps the aspirants could see what Keiji Tachikawa sees: the Palace, Mt. Fuji, and even—he imagines—the countryside of Gifu.

And if they were fortunate enough to speak with the man himself, they might learn that what brought him here, what created at least part of DoCoMo's success, what is even now shaping its future, is a bundle of feelings: the feelings that young Keiji Tachikawa took away from Gifu prefecture all those years ago. Tachikawa packs this powerful mix of emotion, knowledge, and wisdom into a single word: inequality.

The Drive Inside

There is no doubt that feelings of inequality have been a spur for Tachikawa—not to mention for his company and his country. Like yours, like anyone's, his story is unique. But Tachikawa's story also has powerful echoes throughout Japanese business. Those echoes, which have helped him lead DoCoMo to continued success, are feelings of inequality. Some of the inequalities that first lodged in Tachikawa's heart—maybe the most important ones—were personal. Losing the family land "was my first lesson that human beings should be treated on equal footing, and ever since I've been trying to keep this mentality."

Now just imagine what he means by that. An eight-year-old child saw his home taken away, at the insistence of foreigners, to somehow make his country "more democratic." Maybe he was lucky enough to also see familiar people living better than they ever had, because reform had given them land, not taken it away. Still, not many children—not many adults—would store that away as a positive lesson. And though he may not say so in words, surely Tachikawa learned more than the seemingly simple principle that "humans should be treated equally." Perhaps he learned that equal treatment, even if it's the right thing, creates losers as well as winners. Perhaps he found that how much we have is less important than knowing it won't be taken away; that in the world of families and feelings, security matters more than the bottom line. Perhaps he learned that direction is more important than absolute level—that it's not so much how well we live as that we can count on living a little better next year, with no fear of ever living worse.

Box 2-1. Land reform in Japan.

Japan's postwar, American-led land reform has been considered one of the most successful attempts at land redistribution in world history. But a 1999 report by Toshihiko Kawagoe of the World Bank suggests that the positive outcomes were limited or serendipitous. One of the most successful and intended outcomes of land reform was to "democratize" the society so that those actually tilling the land (the tenant farmers) would own the land and could no longer be subjected to the political will of owners of large tracts of land. That part worked. Farming output also increased, but the World Bank report claims that this may have been due to availability of fertilizer (which had been in short supply during the war) and knowledge of new farming techniques.[1]

Certainly, he learned that inequality applies to nations, not just to people. His countrymen had lost a war. Many had also lost a faith they had held since birth; after all, Japan had been led to this place by an emperor—a god on earth. This young boy saw, in the most concrete terms, what national defeat meant. And he had to know that his country lost this war because, on some level, Japan was not equal to the nations of the West. Then, like a generation of children in Europe and Asia during those crucial rebuilding postwar years, Keiji saw every day that his homeland was dominated (benevolently, perhaps, but dominated nonetheless) by legions of foreign men. Finally, as he moved through adolescence into his own manhood, he grew aware of power and inequality on a more abstract level. He learned the ways that nations compete when they are not at war. As Tachikawa began his career, the ocean of experience that he swam in was inequality: the unavoidable economic comparison between Japan and the leading industrial nations—especially the United States.

Economics Is All About Inequality

Inequality may seem like a strange quality to highlight in a book about one of the most successful companies in the world at the turn of this century—especially a business book. At least on this side of the Pacific, we are more accustomed to treating inequality as a social issue. It's a question of law, or policy, not business. But whether we talk about it or not, executives and managers need to be highly aware of inequality. For we would argue that all markets, all of economics, all profitability, and—quite frankly—all business success depends on this difference in levels.

For Tachikawa, the experience of inequality, and its business power, obviously flowed from early childhood. There was the personal contrast between defeated Japanese and victorious, occupying Americans; the steep drop in his own family's station; and, as he looked around him, the undeniable gap in what the two respective countries were able to do. Inequality in power, in economic success, in prosperity, maybe even in happiness—all of that drove him and millions of his countrymen for years. It led them to particular kinds of economic activity. That inequality was the fuel that powered the Japanese economic miracle.

The inequalities that drive other economies are not always quite so obvious. But the power of the inequality is there, almost hydraulic in nature, like the potential energy held in the water behind a dam. We rely on it so instinctively, we hardly notice. But when inequality is not there, we definitely notice.

Mitch remembers as a teenager—admittedly a strange, overly analytical teenager—seeing the difference firsthand. Most of his friends, of course, were from his hometown: a little farming community, twelve thousand people right in the middle of the United States. But Mitch also hung out with friends and teenage relatives who lived in more cosmopolitan settings. We're not talking Manhattan here, or Berlin, but more like Kansas City, or the less glamorous suburbs of Los Angeles. Even so, the contrast was amazing. For his urban friends, things were always changing. They might complain, as adolescents do, that there was nothing going on. But every few months, they could make their complaints in a different teenage hangout, because in the city, new restaurants opened and closed all the time. Even shopaholic teenage girls eventually tired of the mall, but it was always there, with fast-changing stocks in the department stores and a constant supply of new boutiques replacing the ones that hadn't quite made it. And the kinds of things that teens cared about, back then—cars and clothes and music—the city always seemed to have in much greater variety, with some new variation to notice at least once a week.

Back in the farm town, though, nothing changed. Actually, that's not quite right. To be precise:

- Almost nothing changed.

- What did change, changed slowly.

- Very few of the changes stuck for long.

Even in the areas where teens spent time, energy, and money, areas that are fashion driven by definition, most new trends just never made it to Mitch's hometown. The very biggest ones did. But they always came late, in conservative, almost homogenized form. Jumping back and forth between these two adolescent subcultures, it was hard not to see the rural as a pale imitation of the urban. And in most ways, cultural or economic, the imitator never quite got things right. (That has continued, by the way, over the years. Whenever Mitch has visited his hometown, he has seen the kinds of businesses that tend to thrive in cities come and—more quickly—go. Health clubs, bookstores, coffeehouses, restaurants—they're just as appealing, in general, to the people back home as to any city dweller. Every once in a while, someone back home starts such a place. But these upstart businesses—innovations—never last long.)

This never ceased to amaze Mitch—we told you, he was not a normal kid. It mystified him, too. His friends from the city weren't, on average, smarter or more creative or even richer than the ones back home. They didn't seem to care more about all the things they had in greater variety, from fashions to bookstores. So what made the difference?

Box 2-2. The general snubbed?

Many post–World War II analyses of Japan have noted the speed and ease with which the Japanese allowed the United States to oversee the governance of their country. But one of the most telling of those stories, possibly apocryphal, is of General Douglas MacArthur's triumphal motorcade into Tokyo following the end of the war. As the story goes, MacArthur was outraged that the Japanese security forces who lined the streets where his car passed would turn their backs on his car just before he reached their location. He considered this a symbol of the deepest disrespect. A member of the security forces later told him that he had it all wrong. The Americans had won the war; the police were actually "turning their backs" on MacArthur to keep an eye on the crowd and protect the "New Emperor."

> ### Box 2-3. Playing leapfrog?
>
> Many developing countries rely on the theories of later development, second mover advantage, and leapfrog strategies. These theories give hope that less developed or "still developing" countries can eventually play a major role in the world economy.
>
> Certainly Japan has been the inspiring, overpowering example of these theories through the last century. Its success has been so complete, taken for granted now for so many years, that it is easy to forget how unlikely it once seemed.
>
> Before the onset of World War II, Japan had begun to industrialize. But by the end, Allied bombs and wartime priorities had gutted most of the major industrial facilities in the country. Most experts estimated that Japan was thirty or more years behind the other major countries in the world. Imagine traveling today to a country that is thirty years behind the United States. It would seem literally impossible, unthinkable, for that nation to ever really close the gap.
>
> And so it seemed to the world back then. Although Japan was seen as a politically or "strategically" important nation, most discounted the notion that this country would ever play an important economic role.

The answer is inequality. Those cities, whatever their other characteristics, had a lot more of it within their effective borders than the small town did. And that made for huge economic differences.

At first blush, the issue seems to be pure size; more happens in cities because they are bigger. That's true, but it doesn't go far enough. Why does bigger matter? Why does a city of 1 million produce different things—and lots more of them—than the same number of people divided into a hundred little towns? Because it creates more usable inequalities. There are inequalities in assets, in preferences, in information, in social standing. And those inequalities are numerous enough, and in close enough juxtaposition, that you can make money off them. You can, in fact, do what *homo economicus* is supposed to do: Create value out of disparity.

The Classics, Always the Classics

If you think about it, classical economics was all about inequalities, which had always existed: rich and poor, lords and peasants, samurai and farmers, popes and parishioners. Some theorists, like Karl Marx, saw economic disparities as inherently unjust and ultimately destabilizing. Ultimately, they predicted, the repressed proletariat would rise up and quash the landed rich. Many others tried to explain the inequalities away. But everyone understood how much they mattered.

In 1776, Adam Smith explained the rationale for economic markets in terms of division of labor. His point, when you get to the bottom of it, was that it makes sense for producers of goods and services to specialize rather than trying to be self-sufficient *because they are inherently unequal.* Trade, of course, is based on different valuations of the same commodities: 400 rectangles of old but high quality and nicely decorated green paper are worth less to you, today, than a new laser printer; the people at the Brother Corporation or Office Depot feel exactly the opposite. Division of labor, likewise, can be based on people's natural skill sets. (For instance, most of us don't display our artwork at home, but instead pay someone else for their skills in creating works of art.)

Sometimes division of labor is based on repetition and the accompanying acquired skills. Smith's famous example was of a straight pin factory. If a worker made the entire pin, he or she would be less productive than a group of people in which each took one portion of the pin manufacturing process and completed that same task over and over again (one milled the point, another worked on the head of the pin, etc.). This is the basis for production lines and most of modern manufacturing. But it also creates labor markets and markets in general. Each player should do what he or she is best at and then barter those skills for other products and services produced by those who are best at them. Mitch's hometown has so little going on, in part, because there is too little variation in the skills people there have and in their preferences. As he learned when he tried to find summertime jobs, this is a place where lots of people are willing to mow a lawn, and few people are willing to pay to have it done.

Inequality exists among nations, too, of course. Adam Smith didn't much analyze inequalities in regions of the world—and this left an opening half a century later for David Ricardo to propose the theory of comparative advantage in his treatise *On the Principles of Political Economy and Taxation*. Ricardo's theory was that if a country like Portugal can produce both wine and wheat more cheaply than England, then Portugal should do both. But if Portugal can produce wine more cheaply and England is better at wheat, each country should produce to its strengths and trade with the other.

All that assumes, of course, that trade is reasonably easy and inexpensive. That's another way of saying that you need inequalities *among people who can easily barter with one another*. If you're the rare individual with the skill and patience to, say, repair old jukeboxes, you can actually make a living in New York, or Los Angeles, or probably most big cities. Try that in Mitch's hometown, and it will be interesting to see whether you would first starve to death or be laughed out of town. For the customers in the distant city, transportation costs would make you too expensive (even if they could find you out there off the interstate). For the few rural residents who have both the interest and the money to own a jukebox of their own, your prices may well be too high; a lot of people, in a small country town, are willing to try fixing machinery. Snide people might add, "after all, how else will they while away their time out there?"

A Perfect World

Some of modern microeconomics tries to pretend that certain inequalities don't exist. Those alphabet soup economics equations that make so little sense to most of us rely on the notion that there are perfect markets and perfect information. But the fact is that some of the most serious economic "anomalies" in history—stock market crashes, depressions, economic booms—occur exactly because there *are* inequalities in information. We saw the inequalities that drove a couple of economic busts in the last decade—usually they happen when the speculative appeal of a stock, an industry, or a national economy is unreasonably stronger than the underlying structural strength of the same stock, industry or economy (see Boxes 2-4 and 2-5). Huge fortunes are made when the structural strength is actually greater than the speculative appeal.

Sometimes the differential is pure luck: Sutter made lots of money because he homesteaded basically worthless land before there *was* a California gold rush. Other times, it is inequality of information that enables someone to profit from the difference between structural strength and speculative appeal. Samuel Brannan, California's first millionaire, made his fortune from the same gold rush. One of the first to learn that gold had been discovered, he quickly bought up all the supplies and equipment miners would need, opened a general store near the gold fields—and only then began a one-man campaign to publicize the fortunes to be made in mining. The resulting profit margins were measured in multiples, not percent.

Okay, enough about boring economic theories. Think about this in terms of your own life. It has been said that the only things that get a person out of bed in the morning and off to work are fear and greed. You don't have to consider this very long to see that they are *both* about inequality. Greed is because someone else has something that you don't (inequality), and you want it. Fear comes from the idea—in most of us—that others will perform (in reality or by perception of those who pay us) better than we do (again, inequality), and that consequently we will lose our jobs or that the money will go to others.

Drawing on the lessons on the previous pages, from Adam Smith to DoCoMo, we see on pages 52 and 53 five principles managers and executives can use in leveraging inequality to create value.

Box 2-4. Taken for a ride?

Think the Japanese carmakers were an overnight success abroad? Think again. Four years after Toyota first entered the U.S. market, an amazing thing happened—the Japanese car company closed up shop and headed home. It was another four years before they would try again. But their next attempt was much more successful. Japanese automakers went from 0 percent of the U.S. auto market in the mid-1960s to 23 percent by 1991, at the peak of Japan bashing in the United States. On June 30, 1987, members of the U.S. Congress appeared for the press on the Capitol steps, sledge-hammers in hand, to demolish a Japanese-made video recorder.

In 1990, the first President George Bush went to Japan to push for more U.S. car exports. The trip was ill-fated. The famous publicity disaster, of course, occurred when the President threw up in Japanese Prime Minister Miyazawa's lap at a state dinner. The lasting damage, though, came at another phase of the same trip. It, too, was a public relations defeat. It was on this visit that the popular press finally realized that Detroit was trying to sell the Japanese U.S.-made cars with the steering wheels on the wrong side. For the first time, U.S. sentiment turned lukewarm to U.S. carmakers' complaints. Ford, Chrysler, and GM have not made any real inroads into the Japanese market since.

Meanwhile, even in the midst of a recession and a strong yen to dollar ratio, Japanese carmakers have actually increased. And "Buy American" bumper stickers are rare enough to be collectors' items...perhaps because there are ever fewer American bumpers to attach them to.

Box 2-5. Structural strength and speculative appeal.

John and colleague Al Morrison found that the most important lesson from the "Asian financial crisis" of the late 1990s was the profound difference between public perceptions and economic reality. Not only do business leaders often mistake public sentiment and speculative excitement for reality, but government officials also often do not have a firm understanding of the real economic strengths or weaknesses of their country.

A country, for instance, is structurally strong when it serves as a solid base for global business activities and has markets that attract rational, long-term interest by foreign and local investors. Its components include the classical economic factors of land, labor, capital, and entrepreneurship. Abundant usable land, an educated and disciplined workforce, and low-cost capital make countries attractive bases for global companies. Other components include the size and growth of the national economy, the sophistication of consumers, and supportive and enforced government policies.

Speculative appeal, unlike structural strength, is based primarily on perception and opinion, rather than objective measurements. Unlike structural strength, which changes only slowly, speculative appeal can and often does change rapidly. Speculative appeal is fueled by signals that are picked up from various sources, including media sentiment, herd behavior, favorable government policy announcements, and short-term positive changes in financial markets.

In extreme cases, speculative appeal becomes self-generating, taking on a life of its own. A public relations "spin" is created by those who, for whatever reasons, seek to gain from painting an unrealistically rosy future. Governments or private speculators may manipulate press coverage and promote positive policy announcements for their own advantage. No one is immune from speculative appeal, but wise managers seek to dampen its effects by gathering historical data as well as considering present observations. Despite its attractiveness and the ease of collecting information, measurement of speculative appeal cannot serve as a replacement for objective assessment of structural strength. One cannot escape the reality that reliance on speculative appeal is intrinsically risky. It represents at best a gamble on the future.

FIGURE 2-1. Graphing the crisis and its aftermath.

It is easy to visualize the interaction between speculative appeal and structural strength by plotting them on a simple graph. When a "crisis" occurs, as it did in Asia in 1997–1998, there are shifts in the placement of countries in the matrix depicting relationships between structural strength and speculative appeal. These movements are both real and perceived. Speculative appeal, in particular, may change suddenly and dramatically, as illustrated below.

As a result of the Asian crisis, the United States, already in quadrant 4, moved even higher (if that is possible) in terms of both structural strength and speculative appeal. Thailand skidded, from quadrant 2 to quadrant 1, as decreasing confidence in the future and the resultant "mudslide" uncovered the very serious deficiencies in its structural strength. Korea, plagued with many of the same problems, went all the way from quadrant 4 to quadrant 1.

After initial serious bouts of the "Asian Flu," Japan and Taiwan, both of which have relatively strong economies (compared to the rest of

Asia), began to move gradually upward to quadrant 4. Some investors, at least, certainly think so. Although many global companies have been bailing out of Japan (reflected by its weak stock market), some are continuing to make large direct investments in Japan—with more favorable terms than ever available before the Asian financial crisis.

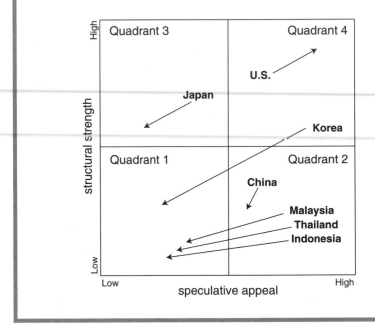

Five principles of inequality:

1. *Inequality makes trade possible.* Wherever you can bring together people who place different values on the same commodity, value can be created. DoCoMo's i-mode service, for instance, literally brought together people who needed, say, subway maps, and other people who had them to sell. Both sets of people existed before, but i-mode made it possible for them to meet, and transact business, at the right moment with almost no overhead cost.

2. *Inequality increases demand.* This can be discounted as keeping up with the Joneses. But, more often, it's a simple phenomenon of learning: Most of us don't know what we want (or need!) until we see it, perhaps in use by someone we can identify with. Getting i-mode out there, on subway trains and into coffeehouses, was critical. The early adopters might not have been mainstream customers, but they were visible.

3. *Inequality drives competition.* We have seen its influence on Tachikawa's life, and on the people of Japan. Or ask any athlete: do you run faster, jump higher, push harder when sincerely doing your best…or when trying to outperform someone else?

4. *Inequality enables innovation.* Seeing systems with different features, in use, enables both producers (like DoCoMo) and customers to decide what they value. The key for the producer is then acting quickly to refine the offering.

5. *Inequality of information creates windfalls.* Despite DoCoMo's huge success, few in the West have even heard of the company. Even in America's nascent wireless data industry and Europe's slightly more advanced version, i-mode's success is not well understood. The first players in these markets who can really understand what lit the i-mode fire, and somehow translate it to their own cultures and markets, may be even more successful. Of course, DoCoMo is busy trying to get there first, worldwide.

The Power of Information and Technology

In this dimension, Tachikawa's feelings were like those of many other Japanese. His have been amplified, though, by at least two factors. First was the pattern that has recurred throughout his working life: long professional stays in the United States. These gave him the time, the settings, and the relationships to really compare his home to the United States. (The first major trip, in the late 1960s, was to visit NASA, where his mission was to learn about satellite technology for NTT.) Second, Tachikawa made his career in a technological field. In his line of work, comparisons are so easy to measure, so central to both the science and the business of telecom, that they just can't be avoided. So at every point, for decades now, he has remained acutely aware of how Japan measures up to leaders in the world market.

As a young man at NTT, Tachikawa quickly learned that this comparison had more than one dimension. For him and his colleagues, the first satellite broadcast to Japan was a milestone. The occasion for this broadcast, as he remembers it, struck him as telling: This satellite link, this triumph of commerce and technology, was transmitting the news that JFK had been assassinated. And it was during Tachikawa's NASA sojourn that Robert Kennedy and Martin Luther King also were killed. He saw America as a deeply troubled place, clearly not the equal, in *this* dimension, of the relatively peaceful and crime-free country that he called home.

At the same time, though, he concluded that the strongest forces underlying American science and industry deserved not only respect, but something near reverence. "From these experiences in the United States, I learned how many ideas and different people there are in the world," Tachikawa says today. "I developed firsthand experiences with equality and individuality."

And, like millions of his contemporaries, Tachikawa focused mainly on the economic comparison. These inequalities—how Japan's wealth, technology, and product quality measured against Western standards—spurred Tachikawa and his company on. For a decade, at least, nearly all he thought about (indeed, nearly all that *anyone* in Japan thought about) was "catching up."

Catching Up

So, fueled by deeply ingrained, nearly permanent feelings of inequality, Tachikawa and his entire generation strove, for years, to catch up. Nowhere in the world did executives and employees work harder. No business culture was more willing to study, to work, and to invest in management ideas and initiatives that promised competitive advantage. And no consumer population had a higher savings rate. It was a sustained time for rebuilding—a time that lasted far longer than the war itself—a unanimous, unspoken national commitment to catching up.

And, of course, it worked. Tachikawa, because of his professional contacts with America, understood this sooner than most. In the mid-1970s, he journeyed to the United States again, this time to work in the New York office of NTT and, as it turned out, to earn a master's degree in business from MIT's Sloan School. During this time it became clear to him that the goal, which had seemed almost eternal, almost *designed* never to be reached, was becoming a reality. He remembers a discussion at MIT where the topic was whether Japan was really *ahead* in some key areas and technologies. The conclusion, from an American perspective, of course, was that "if the United States stayed on the same path it had been on, that would be wrong." As an engineer, Tachikawa had always felt that his work was one of the keys to catching up. He was in the middle of this race for leadership—and the momentum was clearly shifting to his side.

And because he was an engineer, Tachikawa had a glimmer of hope for catching up. It was, after all, technology that in the previous century had helped Japan catch up to an almost 150-year deficit with the modern industrial powers of the time (Europe and the United States). Japan had refused to open its borders to foreign countries in 1853, when U.S. Commodore Matthew C. Perry's "Black Ships" forced the issue in Yokohama. This foreign intervention was the catalyst for truly historic change. The feudalistic Tokugawa Period gave way to Emperor Meiji in 1868 and a wholehearted embrace of all things new and all things Western. Steam power, machines, photography, and electric power all flooded into Japan. By the turn of the century, Japan was considered almost "caught up."

After another thirty years, the Japanese military establishment decided it was actually ahead of most other countries and able to include much of Asia in the Empire. Although the political and military aggression brought bitter results, the rapid growth that had made the aggression possible provided a lasting lesson. Tachikawa, the engineer, knew how far Japan had come—and how quickly!—when it had embraced technology in the past. He had good reason to hope that technology would play a major role in helping his country to catch up again.

How Does Inequality Create Success?

There is no doubt that Japan lagged behind the United States through the 1950s and 1960s in terms of economic strength. World War II and the rebuilding period immediately after had seriously damaged Japan. In the early 1990s, experts estimated that Japan's aircraft building industry (which had been world class during the war) was at least a decade behind the West. When you think about the assets and capabilities that Japan started with, back before the war, this is a huge gap. After all, the nation was known for great engine and airframe technology in the 1940s; Mitsubishi had built the Zero fighter planes. But following the war, the U.S. occupation forces prohibited Japanese firms from doing any aircraft building. For seven years, the country was stopped from developing technology and skills. So the kind of process and know-how refinements that have moved Japanese automakers to the top of the international rankings simply didn't happen. The result is an aircraft industry in Japan that does some subcontracting to Boeing and Airbus, but that will not, in the foreseeable future, be able to build a large passenger aircraft on its own.[2]

Second Mover Advantages

In other industries—the ones that were not prohibited, the ones where General MacArthur and the Marshall Plan actually encouraged immediate rebuilding—the inequality engendered by the war was not nearly so disastrous. In steel, automobiles, and consumer electronics, as a matter of fact, the United States created its own strongest competitor. In these industries, U.S. companies have had considerable competition from Japan—in some cases, losing huge chunks of market share. Although Japanese steel is no longer competitive, auto and electronics are still the country's major exporters. And the success of these industries can be blamed almost exclusively on inequality.

The U.S. bombings in World War II had targeted Japanese steel-making plants. Following the war, Japan rebuilt these steel mills

> ## Box 2-6. W. Edwards Deming.
>
> Quality control—including the work of Wyoming-born W. Edwards Deming—has been part of the U.S. business landsape for nearly two decades now. But the Japanese had adopted the processes (and the guru) thirty years earlier. Deming was well into middle age when he first went to Japan in 1950 almost a quarter century after getting his Ph.D. in mathematical physics at Yale. He had worked during World War II at the Census Bureau and tried to teach U.S. firms about the importance of quality control, but no one listened much. In Japan he found a much more receptive audience—an audience willing to listen to an American about a topic on which they felt somewhat inferior and unequal: quality (see Box 2-7).
>
> The results of the quality revolution were slow to emerge. A decade after Deming won the Emperor's Second Order Medal of the Sacred Treasure in 1960 (the first American to win the award) for the help he was giving Japanese firms, Mitch and John, like pretty much every American kid, understood that when adults said "made in Japan," that was code for cheap, low-quality goods—probably bad copies of something made in the U.S.A. But during the 1970s, that arrogance suffered a rapid and painful about-face, as the quality and innovation of Japanese work came back to haunt the U.S. economy in steel, autos, and electronics. Surprisingly, it was 1980 before Deming was "discovered" in the United States—as part of an NBC documentary called "If Japan Can…Why Can't We?"

> ### Box 2-7. More management than statistics.
>
> Deming's real contribution to management theory was not that statistics should be used in business, but that everyone (not just the statisticians) should use statistics. Promotions, bonuses, and all communications between management and workers should be based on these numbers. That way, he explained, everyone is working toward the same goal—a goal that is objective and easy to compare over time.

from scratch, which meant that their steel mills were more modern by decades than their U.S. counterparts. Those decades had produced many innovations in the production of steel itself and in the machinery and physical plants to make the steel. The Japanese were able to incorporate all of these ideas into their new operations.[3]

"The Japanese could build a 747 on their own today, but it would take ten years to complete and cost many times the amount that it cost Boeing."

—AIRCRAFT MANUFACTURING EXPERT

In automobiles, the Japanese succeeded partly for the same reason that steel was successful, because the plants were newer. But there is more to this story than just new facilities—the Japanese adopted new "American" quality processes that its rivals in the United States were unwilling to take on. By the 1990s, "quality control" had achieved acceptance in the United States, and homegrown gurus like Deming, who had been ignored in their native land for years, were finally recognized for their work. By then, however, inequality had moved to the other foot.

Box 2-8. Second mover advantages.

During the 1940s, both CBS and RCA were developing a color television system. The FCC adopted the CBS system in 1950. But during the Korean War the production of color TVs was suspended because materials were needed for the war effort. During that time RCA kept improving its technology while CBS rested on its "standards" laurels.

By 1953, RCA had improved its color technology significantly and it petitioned the National Television System Committee (NTSC) to review its decision. The Committee agreed. RCA color televisions went into production in March 1954. Today the U.S. standard is still RCA—known around the world as the NTSC standard.

A little extra time, a more developed competitive technology, and some luck—in the form of a war—was all it took to put RCA on top.

Taking What No One Else Wants

In both steel and automobiles, Japan was taking advantage of all of the classic second mover advantages (see Box 2-8). But the Japanese caught up with and surpassed the United States in consumer electronics for second-mover reasons...and yet another reason—the U.S. inventors and pioneers gave the industry to them. U.S. manufacturers of radios, televisions, and stereos all could see that their industries were becoming commodity businesses, so they decided to get out. The Japanese were low-cost producers and were willing to pay for licenses. So these U.S. companies first moved production to Japan and then sold whole companies to Japanese entities. Before we knew it, there was no way to buy a radio made by a U.S. company. We had let the second movers have the industry.

Trade Wars Swing Like a Pendulum Do?

Given these patterns, it is probably not surprising that technologists like Tachikawa were among the first to see the signs of the closing distance. But the world soon noticed. In 1979, Harvard's Ezra Vogel published *Japan As Number One*. Vogel was the first to explain how Japan posed a very real threat to what Americans and Europeans still took for granted: Western dominance of the global economy. His book

---

Box 2-9. Steel production in 1998.

Country	Production (Million Tons)
People's Republic of China	114.3
United States	97.7
Japan	93.5
Former USSR	74.4
Germany	44.0
Korea	39.9
Brazil	25.8
India	23.5
rest of world	261.3
World Total	**774.4**

SOURCE: INTERNATIONAL IRON AND STEEL INSTITUTE.

became a bestseller in the United States and a runaway hit in Japan. It forced both sides to acknowledge a fact that, for very different reasons, they had been reluctant to see: Japan had finally caught up.

In fact, the pendulum of perception—and perhaps market reality—swung even further. By the late 1980s, when Tachikawa returned to New York City, Japan was actually seen as surpassing the United States. In his judgment, there was definitely overreaction. "As far as management style, not all Japanese companies were strong in the 1980s and 1990s like Americans seemed to believe—some were good, some were not." He also believes that, at least during the 1970s and 1980s, Japan had enjoyed the advantages of not leading. "Japan lags behind the United States by ten years; changes are slower here. So Japan has had an easy model—it was good to be behind. All Japan had to do was follow."

Still, during his three years at the helm of NTT's U.S. office, Tachikawa faced daily reminders that leaders in American politics and business saw his own organization and many of its peers as something close to national enemies. NTT, among others, was targeted by Congress and U.S. firms for "unfair" trade practices. It felt like Japan was out ahead. The problem had shifted radically—but feelings of inequality were still driving it all.

An Elusive Opponent

Just as Tachikawa and his countrymen were beginning to master this new game of seesaw competition with the United States, where the competitive balance could go either way—with hazards for Japan no matter which end was up—the game changed entirely. Despite the truly historic triumphs that Japanese business had won during his lifetime, Tachikawa now saw his nation's entire economy overcome, not by a technological or business competitor, but by the abstract, invisible, almost impenetrable forces of macroeconomics. Japan entered a recession that, a decade later, still lingers.

In Tachikawa's view, that recession was a natural outgrowth of the Japanese triumph—maybe even inevitable. "It is not surprising that depression set in after the Japan bubble burst. The stagnation of the current period was expected." That is, after decades of the Japanese working hard and saving fanatically, all in order to "catch up," their economy at long last had achieved a huge, globally recognized success. This triumph—which truly has few, if any, parallels in all of economic history—created a certain amount of euphoria. Add to that an enormous supply of cash, from all that work and all that saving. Then factor in typical market overreaction, only this time on a worldwide scale: With modern mass communications and the emerging global economy, literally everyone on the planet who had money to invest knew about the Japanese juggernaut, and wanted to get a piece of it (if only to hedge against the threat of stagnating Western economies). What you had, then, was a powerful formula for overvaluing Japanese assets.

And there's simply no question that the formula worked. When you can theoretically sell the city of Tokyo and with the proceeds buy all the land in California (roughly the same land mass as all of Japan), you know you've got a problem—no matter what your taste in coun-

FIGURE 2-2. Rents in Tokyo and Atlanta: 1987–2000.

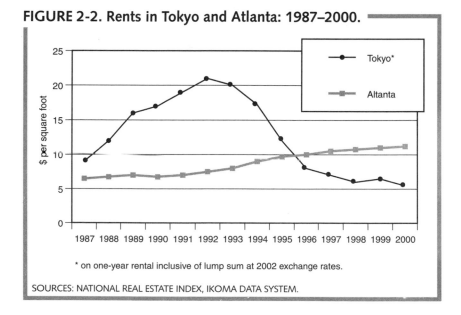

* on one-year rental inclusive of lump sum at 2002 exchange rates.

SOURCES: NATIONAL REAL ESTATE INDEX, IKOMA DATA SYSTEM.

tries, cultures, or cuisines. When the market corrected, as it always eventually does, Japan's economy hit recession. Long-standing problems in the structure of Japanese financial institutions and the transparency of their markets compounded the slide. So Japan's recession is with us still.

Tachikawa, however, hopes that this difficult phase is now essentially over. "People really needed the time to think about why the bubble happened, why it burst, and how to overcome those problems and grow again," he says. But "the last decade has been a *long* period of reflection. The readjustment has gone on long enough." From his perspective, the Japanese economy is now ready: ready both psychologically (the human attitudes that drive markets have come full circle) and numerically (the relative values of Japanese assets compared to U.S. and European counterparts are such that a reasonable growth rate in Japan makes economic sense).

Playing with a Handicap

Whether it is over yet or not, Japan's long economic contraction has been a fact of DoCoMo's life for as long as DoCoMo has had a life. If you want to understand just how rare the DoCoMo story is, this tells you more than any academic study you can imagine: In the midst of a deep recession, in a hypercompetitive sector filled by huge international players, a sleepy monopoly (practically part of the government itself) spun off not only a successful new firm, but a market leader. And, with i-mode, this competitor has been able to achieve success in a market—mobile data—where billions have been invested and yet where, even in 2002, no one else had really made it work.

Many, many factors combined to yield this unexpected success. Tachikawa himself emphasizes that the single most important element is the leadership of Chairman Ohboshi. "He is the big success factor; my job is just to keep the current levels going and to further improve them." Fair enough, yet how can the company's CEO *not* have been a factor? Indeed, a close look at DoCoMo's history reveals that Tachikawa has been a vital player as well. And all along, this player has used feelings of inequality to inspire himself and his colleagues.

Missing the Brake

"Inspiration" wasn't the word that came to mind when Tachikawa first joined DoCoMo. Because he was a lifelong NTTer known for relatively conservative views, many in the press expected that his appointment

---

Box 2-10. The most valuable firms.

Even as Japan's entire stock market declined sharply in value (by 70 percent between the early 1990s and the first years of the new millennium), NTT DoCoMo became one of the ten top wealth-creating firms in the world—one of just three not based in the United States, and the only one from Asia.

Stern Stewart created the Wealth Added Index (WAI), which compares share-price increases and dividends to the cost of equity for 5,069 companies between June 1996 and June 2001. Here are the top ten:

Rank	Company	Country	Wealth added ($Billion)
1	General Electric	U.S.	$227
2	Microsoft	U.S.	$150
3	Mannesmann	Germany	$121
4	Wal-Mart Stores	U.S.	$118
5	Citigroup	U.S.	$113
6	IBM	U.S.	$107
7	Nokia	Finland	$85
8	AIG	U.S.	$81
9	NTT DoCoMo	Japan	$79
10	AOL Time Warner	U.S.	$68

was designed to moderate the spinoff. Some even speculated that his mission was specifically to "rein in" the renegade firm, serving as a human brake on the new company's more aggressive thinking.

The speculators were surprised. With Tachikawa, DoCoMo got not a brake but a turbocharger. Far from suppressing innovation, he quickly became the biggest cheerleader of creative, aggressive solutions. In late 2001 he announced that he planned to increase the penetration of DoCoMo handsets in Japan to 500 percent of the Japanese population by extending the functionality to machines and to pets. A quirky vision? Perhaps. But it quickly and memorably made the point, to DoCoMo and to the market, that traditional thinking about this market was simply too small. Far from being a conservative box-checker, Tachikawa forced his firm to think outside the box. Like other Big Hairy Audacious Goals (see Box 2-11), the vision of 500 percent DoCoMo penetration may never be achieved.[4] But the firm has done amazing things because that goal was articulated.

Although this may have surprised the pundits at the watercooler, given Tachikawa's history and values, it makes perfect sense. As he reflects on the contributions that DoCoMo hopes to make, the same themes emerge: a belief in technology, a deep understanding of the global market, and—most of all—those feelings of inequality. These forces don't necessarily contradict the conservative decisions so common in large Japanese companies. Rather, for an organization placed like DoCoMo, they simply apply more visibly. As a leader of a company, Tachikawa says, "You have to look to the future and forget about the glories of the past." There are times in history, he points out, when information technology simply forces that approach. The printing press and the telephone made major changes, over a long period of time. He fully expects mobile communications, both voice and data, to do the same.

Techno Super-Friends

The companies that will lead in such a period of change, he says, are those that "develop new fields of business, improve technology, and strengthen their existing management styles; and of course, the very foundation of management philosophy has to be a solid one." The key to doing all that, he believes, is to focus on fostering equality—and constant progress—for all people. "To become a leader, any business must have a solid philosophy. It must think not just about profits and making money, but mostly about people. Printing technology made a huge contribution to people's thinking processes." It became one of the Truly Big Things in economic history, he says, because "it made it easier for people to think, to consider things more." The telephone followed the same pattern. "The year 1890 was the first time for telephones—developments have followed for the next century."

━━━

Alexander Bell started hawking his new invention, the telephone, immediately after its invention, but it was two years before the first switchboard was installed—with eight subscribers. Bell's recommendation that the phone should be answered with the word "Ahoy" never caught on. The moral of this story? No one hits a home run every time, not even certified geniuses. But they always swing with style, don't they? As Jerry Seinfeld might say, "Ahoy??!!??"

━━━

Drawing on such models, Tachikawa long ago formulated his principles for technology and business. "I believe in a society improved by technological advancement." For an information technology company to succeed by becoming part of that process, it must have a simple goal: "to make life more comfortable, more convenient, and to support people's thinking lives." Mobile communications can clearly do that, and Japan is poised to lead the change. Tachikawa is the first to point out that his nation and his company do not lead the world in every relevant technology. But he notes that in two key areas of telecommunications, fiber optics and digital microwave, "Japan has strong capabilities." (Modestly, he does not mention either DoCoMo or NTT.) The opportunity, he believes, is there for DoCoMo to take.

Tachikawa believes that DoCoMo is the Microsoft of mobile communications. By that, he doesn't simply mean that "we can be a big success." Neither does he mean that DoCoMo will become a global household name. He has something different, and quite specific, in mind. Tachikawa expects that, over the next few years, services like i-mode will finally emerge around the world. With the help of DoCoMo's global partner network, he expects that most of those services will involve i-mode itself—at the very least as the basis of a business model or as a vital and value-added technology backbone.

But the goal is not to be a brand name in the way that the other large Japanese companies are. Though he respects Sony and Matsushita, he has no plans to emulate them. Rather, his goal for DoCoMo is to maintain the top market capitalization in Japan. Also, not surprisingly, he seeks financial results that "achieve comparable levels with Europe and the United States." In his view, DoCoMo's financials today are a lot like the balance sheets of other Japanese companies...just bigger and achieved in fewer years. Tachikawa argues that there is a much higher bar for financial success in the rest of the world—and that Japan can measure up to this standard.

Sensing Success

Tachikawa believes that Japan can address this new level of inequality and take a new position in the global economy. No longer running to catch up, nor intimidating trading partners, Japan instead can play a less confrontational role: creating growth by concentrating on its unique gifts and capabilities. Japan's success, under this model, would fall in the win/win category. To make DoCoMo a leader in this transformation, he will look to the same deep forces he has always relied on: the power of science and technology to make people's lives better, and the firm's ability to help individuals, families, and other companies achieve their own equality with these tools. To Tachikawa, this is just the next logical step in a process that has the scale, and force, of history.

"Cell phones were a big change. They made people's lives a lot easier." His company has achieved remarkable growth because "DoCoMo enabled people to communicate on the move with a wireless device during the 1990s." The coming transformation will depend

FIGURE 2-3. Japanese technology adoption curves.

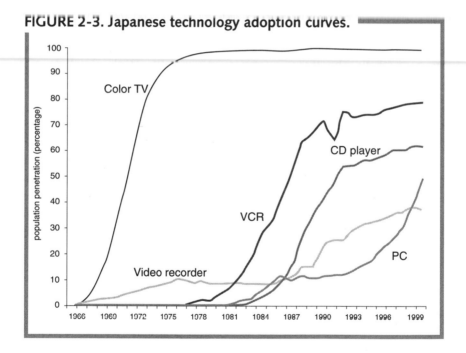

on an equally striking advance. Tachikawa calls it "3D Virtual Reality Communications." He notes that today's technology, though it is called multimedia, tends to rely primarily on one sense (either sight or sound), and almost never to weave multiple senses together in the way that real life, and many artistic experiences, do.

FIGURE 2-4. Top twenty Japanese companies
by market capitalization.*

Rank	Company Name	Market Cap (100 million yen)
1	NTT DoCoMo	138,497
2	Toyota	131,400
3	NTT	63,732
4	Sony	57,211
5	Honda	53,300
6	Takeda Chemical Industries	49,444
7	Mitsubishi Tokyo Financial Group	46,443
8	Canon	38,469
9	Matsushita	36,538
10	TEPCO	35,851
11	Seven Eleven	33,565
12	Mitsui-Sumitomo Bank	32,648
13	Nomura Securities	30,275
14	Nissan	29,989
15	Nintendo	29,467
16	Hitachi	29,307
17	Mizuho Holdings	25,287
18	East Japan Railways	23,600
19	Fuji Photo Film	23,364
20	ROHM	20,961

*As of March 2002.

Tachikawa believes that now, however, the imminent rollout of 3G technology finally gives DoCoMo the power to break out of single-sense communications. He wants future versions of i-mode to supply three of the five human senses (sight, sound, and touch) through a communications device. That combination, "virtual substance transmission," would change the game as deeply as mobile data has, and mobile voice before it. It would open the way for a set of applications and services that, like the content providers that have fueled i-mode's success, cannot be imagined in advance.

Another of Tachikawa's quirky and aggressive BHAGs? (See box 2-11.) Perhaps. But, like that earlier goal of 500 percent penetration, it

---

Box 2-11. BHAGs.

"BHAG," which is short for Big Hairy Audacious Goal, comes from the book, *Built to Last: Successful Habits of Visionary Companies* (see note 4). As the name implies, a BHAG is a bold mission, boldly proclaimed, and pursued with bold commitment. Its value is to stimulate progress. We believe that it works by resetting the expectations of employees, by demonstrating and thus spreading confidence, and by keeping everyone focused on the company's overall goal. As authors James Collins and Jerry Porras point out, it typically seems much bolder to those outside the company than to those inside. After all, the insiders—as at DoCoMo—already know what they can do.

Our favorite example, perhaps because it seems almost as crazy as Tachikawa's 500 percent market penetration, is one of Sam Walton's BHAGs. In 1990, Walton set a specific target of $125 billion in annual sales. At that time, the biggest retailer on the planet had annual sales of $30 billion. Only one corporation, GM, had volume anywhere close to Walton's target. Twelve years later, Wal-Mart's annual sales were $217 billion. Perhaps 500 percent i-mode penetration isn't so far off after all.

focuses all of us on a future for wireless data that is far outside the box—one that might inspire consumers, employees, investors, and content creators to take the kind of leaps that got DoCoMo, and modern Japan, to where it is today. After all, Tachikawa says "my goal is to change the lifestyle of people with cell phones." Even if his vision is never precisely realized, it seems sure to inspire the kind of dramatic impact he is seeking.

* * * * *

In a way, Tachikawa's visions are just highly memorable, visible, dramatic scenarios to remind DoCoMo staff and managers of key inequalities—the gap between what the product could be and what it is; the gap between DoCoMo and the competition; the gap between the success they now enjoy and the larger success they seek. Other lessons from this master of managing inequality:

■ *If you are not in first place, no matter how great the distance seems, you can make it up.* And whenever you find yourself in first place...watch out. Someone as hungry, resourceful, and resolute as postwar Japan probably has you in their sights.

■ *Leapfrogging is not just for kids.* Japan had the advantage of brand-new factories—an advantage created by starting out so far behind. DoCoMo had the disadvantage of a nonexistent market—and leapfrogged it by inventing an entirely new kind of product, which put it ahead of competitors worldwide. A competitor today, for instance, can draw lessons from the Internet as well as from more traditional telecomm markets—lessons that some competitors will ignore because they seem too far afield.

■ *Being second can be fantastic motivation.* In the United States, Avis is famous for trying harder. Tachikawa and his contemporaries took that strategy to a very successful extreme.

■ *When leapfrogging, use the infrastructure that does exist.* DoCoMo was able to take advantage of the existing DoPa network infrastructure for i-mode (DoPa is a PDC pocket network which over-laid DoCoMo's conventional PDC network and became operational in 1997). This had technical costs, and certainly political ones. But it let the company leap forward quickly, concentrating its resources else-where.

The key lesson: Find the emotion that is best at moving you for-ward, as Tachikawa did. Don't simply use it, but feed it (as he did with trips to the United States and with technology comparisons). If you are fortunate enough to share key values with your team, see how far that internal motivation will take you.

Notes

1. Toshihiko Kawagoe, "Agricultural Land Reform and Postwar Japan: Experi-ences and Issues, *World Bank Report*, May 1999.

2. Asian Business Information, *The Japanese Aircraft Industry*, 1990.

3. William Scheuerman, *The Steel Crisis: The Economics and Politics of a Declin-ing Industry* (New York: Praeger Publishers, 1986).

4. James C. Collins and Jerry I. Porras, *Built to Last: Successful Habits of Visionary Companies* (New York: HarperBusiness, 1994).

CHAPTER THREE

Impatience

"Patience, the beggar's virtue, shall find
no harbour here."

—PHILIP MASSINGER

AT FIRST GLANCE, Kouji Ohboshi seems like a conventional Japanese executive at the highest levels. He certainly looks the part: gray hair, high-quality but conservative suits, and relatively tall (as so many business leaders in Japan somehow end up being). His manner, too, is what you would expect of a major international firm's founding CEO, ascended now to corporate chairman. A Westerner would probably describe him as distinguished, highly analytical, absolutely professional—but not precisely warm. The overall reading is impressive, and not at all surprising. Yet the underlying reality *is* a surprise, even a shock. It doesn't take long to realize that there is nothing conventional about Ohboshi's thinking—or his actions.

Clues are apparent even before you meet. Staff people and press officers casually mention that he is "something of a character." They note that people interviewing the chairman don't usually need to say much. Without meaning to, they show their concern that no nervous tics will manifest themselves. They call, repeatedly, to increase the time allotted. And when they make those calls, it doesn't sound as if other commitments are simply dropping away from the calendar, leaving the chairman with time to fill. Rather, you can almost picture him, thinking in odd moments: "and I'll need to explain this part of our history; better arrange for fifteen extra minutes to cover that"; then, the command given, switching instantly to one of dozens of other issues that will receive the same intense focus and immediate action. Eventually, these glimpses of the inner Ohboshi converge to outline an unusual pattern: a corporate leader at the highest levels who is still extremely hands on, personally involved in the details, with a remarkably fertile mind—and a powerful control streak.

Once you spend time with Chairman Ohboshi, that outline is filled in with vibrant colors, and the driving energy that created the pattern becomes clear. At the core is a profound, thoughtful impatience. This is not the surface excitement of the classic type A. It is not nervousness. (Despite earlier hints, there are no visible tics, though his press people remain wary, constantly watching for—what? a tapping foot?) And it is not a rude or imperious attitude. Ohboshi projects exactly the same assurance that virtually all traditional Japanese leaders do: an unwavering certainty that whatever course he chooses is the way things will be. But it is all done with grace.

No, the impatience that clearly drives Ohboshi is much deeper, a combination of energy and focus that simply won't make time for any delay. This chairman is fully capable of (and known for) talking for an hour and a half before the interviewer says, literally, one word. He goes fast because he is covering a lot of ground—and doing it in great depth. His Japanese is difficult to translate, not only because he uses the rather formal speech of his generation, but because his *thinking* is compact, incredibly efficient. He uses *Yoji-jukugo*, little four-syllable proverbs that are very ancient. They are almost impossible to translate because they condense so much meaning from history and context into such a tiny package. Likewise, though it's not his training, Chairman Ohboshi speaks the language of economics—another field where huge chunks of analysis and past experience are compressed into short phrases. (Just try explaining "economies of scale" to someone who has never taken economics; the concepts are not difficult, but there are lots of layers implied in those three words. Now imagine a conversation where most phrases are that densely packed—and a lot more obscure.)

Skimming over the analytic landscape at this speed, Ohboshi can easily leave others behind. And his inclination is to keep moving. He knows what the enterprise needs and goes directly to it, without stopping for possible diversions. It's a pattern evident throughout his career. It is why, before he became chairman, he dubbed himself *gokiburi shacho* ("cockroach president").

Cockroach President?

What does a cockroach president do? To Chairman Ohboshi, it is obvious. He does what highly intelligent and equally impatient people always do: He scurries around getting into everything around him. In sharp contrast to virtually all executives in Japan (and most in the rest of the world), he doesn't wait for a network of others to find out what is in the environment. He does not pause for consensus to build. He goes out and discovers for himself what is happening "on the ground." He instantly decides—not by impulse, but through rapid thought—on a response. And he begins, immediately, making things happen.

Ohboshi's "cockroach" style is so direct that, in the old DoCoMo headquarters, he became known for scurrying up and down the back staircases. This is not conventional for a senior Japanese executive. The narrow-minded might call it bizarre. But it was the fastest way for him to reach all the floors of the company and connect immediately with employees at all levels, day and night. DoCoMo's new building inadvertently discourages this pattern; the security system prevents anyone, even the chairman, from re-entering the work spaces once he is in the emergency stairs. Although architectural details can change, the chairman's style shows signs of being more permanent. One employee remembers hearing a frantic knocking from the fire escape one night at the new headquarters. When she opened the door, there was the chairman—locked in the stairwell and facing the prospect of a forty-story walk down to street level to escape.

Ohboshi's impatience creates great stories for the rank and file. But its effects go much further; every DoCoMo partner, investor, and employee has that impatience to thank for the company's unparalleled success. As his successor, Keiji Tachikawa points out, DoCoMo's success is largely a product of Ohboshi's vision. It was Ohboshi who envisioned the potential for a successful wireless spin-off from NTT and tirelessly drove the company into unknown areas that happened to be very profitable. Three times during the young company's history, DoCoMo has faced real crises. In each case, his impatient drive has brought the firm through, not only alive, but stronger than before. Even deeper, we believe that impatience is the answer to the toughest riddle of NTT DoCoMo's success: *How can an innovative, history-making startup like DoCoMo emerge from a stodgy, protected monopoly like NTT?*

*   *   *   *   *

Ohboshi began his career in 1957, after graduating in law from Japan's top educational institution, Tokyo University. Like many of his classmates, he saw the law degree as a stepping stone—but not to the practice of law. He might have considered a career in the political bureaucracy. Many of his friends did. Government service was seen as the most noble profession at the time—a value judgment fueled both by a planned economy, just emerging from the ravages of war, and by a Confucian philosophy that placed public servants at the top of the prestige hierarchy and merchants at the bottom. But for Ohboshi, there was a natural attraction to business. So he chose to join a different bureaucracy, a quasi-government agency itself: Nippon Telegraph and Telephone Public Corporation (NTT).

Once inside NTT, Ohboshi rose through the ranks like everyone else. This was still the Japan of lifetime employment at a single company. With no mid-career hiring, it was easy—practically automatic—to put everyone on similar tracks after college. Like most large organizations in Japan at that time, NTT made a point of keeping all of its employees in lockstep for the first ten years or so of their careers. It was only when an employee neared the level of *kacho* (manager), in his mid-thirties, that differences in salary and position were allowed to emerge.

Typically, the vast majority of any given intake "class" would be promoted to *kacho* at the same time. But a small percentage would be promoted a year early, and another even smaller group a year late. Ohboshi-san was certainly not relegated to that shameful, bottom group. But neither was he promoted to *kacho* early. Instead, he was left in the great, undifferentiated middle, becoming *kacho* along with virtually everyone else in his cohort—hardly predictive of a man who would later become founding CEO, then chairman of a firm that would open a new future for Japanese business in the midst of a ten-year recession.

Ohboshi's first indication that he was destined for something more than a typical career path came in 1984, when he was made the associate vice president/director of Chugoku Telecommunications Bureau. This was promising—though hardly spectacular, and certainly not decisive. His next promotion, to executive vice president of business strategy, was more encouraging. But neither he nor NTT's leadership could have foreseen how this post set him up for a move that would change, not just his life, but Japan's economic prospects.

The 1980s were the heyday of "Japan, Inc." Leaders in the United States and Europe—business and government alike—feared that their nations simply could not compete with Japan's combination of obsessive workers, modern factories, unfailing quality, patient capital, hardwired government cooperation, and what often seemed like unfair trade practices. In addition, Japan's increasing wealth made it ever more vital as a market. So by the late 1980s and early 1990s, NTT was under enormous pressure from American (and to some extent, European) politicians. Telecommunications companies like AT&T and MCI wanted a piece of Japan's lucrative telecommunications sector. Manufacturers like Motorola and Nortel got into the act as well, trying to sell equipment to Japan. These companies were large and important enough to attract serious attention from their own national governments. Those governments, in turn, pressured Japan. In the case

Box 3-1. Confucian job hierarchy.

The early shogun rulers in Japan cleverly drew on Confucian values (already in place in Japan) to create a very strict class system based on profession.

- At the top of the system was the government bureaucracy (*bakufu*).

- Next came the group that policed and kept order in society, the samurai.

- Then, the populace had to be fed, so farmers were important.

- Craftsmen were very close to farmers in status—this was generally a catch-all level in the hierarchy for anyone in the peasant class who didn't farm. (Usually performers fell into this class, but some Kabuki and Noh actors actually were treated much more like *daimyo*, great lords.)

- Far below anyone else in mainstream society were the merchants. They grew rich, lived in nice homes, and gave financial support to samurai and the government officials, but because they profited from the labors of others, they fell at the bottom of the chain.

But even below merchants were a group known as *burakumin* or "untouchables." This group worked in "unclean" jobs like leather tanning or butchering. Even today, some potential marriage partners run background checks on their betrothed to make sure that their families do not hail from the *burakumin* class.

of NTT, the approach that the U.S. government advocated was, naturally, a Japanese version of the solution they had imposed on their own telecommunications giant: deregulation and breakup.

This "baby-Bell" approach was not at all attractive to NTT. So the firm searched frantically for less drastic kinds of deregulation. The strategy group, which Ohboshi now headed, was constantly involved in discussions and analysis of proposals intended to help NTT dodge the ax—or at least convince deregulators to use a scalpel instead. Eventually, the Japanese government decided that an NTT "spin-off" of some business lines would result in a slimmed down, less powerful central company, thus allowing greater opportunity for Western competitors.

One of the biggest chunks spun off was the nascent NTT Mobile Communications Network. By Global 500 standards, the NTT unit was, at that point, hardly more than a concept. And the Japanese mobile phone market was widely seen as a bust. Although Japan had led the world in introducing this technology—the first modern car phone was introduced there in 1979, and Japan was the pioneer in offering cellular (as opposed to radio band) phone service—uptake was very slow. In the country's first thirteen years of cellular phone sales, only 1 million people had adopted the new technology. Not many of Ohboshi's peers were excited about a tiny market averaging just 80,000 new users per year.

So when he was asked to take over as the spin-off's first CEO, it must have seemed a mixed blessing, at best. On the one hand, this move signaled, unmistakably, that Ohboshi was not in line for the highest levels inside the parent company, NTT. (It is tempting to imagine the senior discussions that took place—as they presumably had at other turning points in his NTT career—with Ohboshi receiving praise for his keen intelligence...along with the inevitable reservations about his impatience.) And while CEO of *anything* is a plum, of sorts, NTT's expectations for the mobile spin-off were not particularly high.

In the real world of customers and revenue, mobile at that time meant car phones, which seemed like a niche almost by definition. Statistically, mobile was a *micro*-niche, at just 1 percent of the population. So the suggestion that he head this new company had to have left him a little cold.

But Ohboshi was able to see past these offsetting factors, to the big game that lay beyond. His vantage point as head of strategic planning had given him the data to understand that mobile communications in Japan was poised to take off. Equally important, his quick and impatient mind allowed him to envision this future, not yet blessed as part of conventional wisdom. (Even when they have invested large sums in R&D, large organizations—especially those that are so successful or protected that they can *afford* to focus inward—almost inevitably discount any venture that doesn't fit neatly into "the way things are done here.") Ohboshi understood that the sale of Motorola StarTAC phones in Japan was creating a new interest in mobile communications; that handsets were finally becoming small enough to really appeal to a Japanese consumer; and that although it was only a million-unit market, Japanese customers had purchased 300,000 cell phones in the previous year.

FIGURE 3-1. Pre-breakup comparison of AT&T and NTT.

	AT&T (1982)	NTT (1993)
Assets	$150 billion	$140 billion
Number of customers	70 million	58 million
Employees	1 million	250,000
Net income	$7 billion	$810 million
Access lines	140 million	56 million
Population served	250 million	125 million
Territory size	9.37 million km²	378,000 km²

SOURCE: RICHARD E. NOHE, "A DIFFERENT TIME, A DIFFERENT PLACE: BREAKING UP TELEPHONE COMPANIES IN THE UNITED STATES AND JAPAN," *FEDERAL COMMUNICATION LAW JOURNAL*, INDIANA UNIVERSITY, MARCH 1996.

And he foresaw that this trend would go much further. He believed that here was a chance to really get in on the ground floor of a great opportunity. There was another factor, too: impatience. The same emotion that had presumably kept Ohboshi from certain promotions made him willing to take this very real risk. In 1992 Kouji Ohboshi agreed to be the first president of NTT Mobile Communications Network, Incorporated—the company that became DoCoMo and that, with i-mode, delivered the most successful new product introduction, ever perhaps, reaching 30 million customers in just over three years.

CRISIS 1
The Case of the Unhappy Customers

Ohboshi's first two years as CEO—DoCoMo's first two years of life— were not happy ones. With the bursting of the Japanese bubble economy, cell phone sales slumped. In his first eighteen months, the company sold only half as many handsets as it had in the twelve months before spin-off. For the employees of the newly independent company, this was naturally a time of great stress. For their entire careers, they had been part of *the* telecommunications utility in Japan. Lifetime employment was formally assured, regular growth in services was almost guaranteed, and one could always plan on a healthy year-end bonus.

Ohboshi recalls this as the first time in his thirty-year career when he had been worried. His people were afraid that they were on a listing ship—and Ohboshi had to find a way to make sure it didn't go under. He remembers going out to drink with his subordinates and watching them literally weep into their sake as they expressed their worries. At the company housing complex, he heard the children of his employees singing out a new jump rope rhyme: "DoCoMo wa Doko?" (Where is DoCoMo?). He felt like he was on the edge of a very steep precipice. How did Ohboshi respond? Naturally, by growing impatient.

For some leaders, being on the edge of a very frightening thought somehow ignites their passion. It's as if they handle intense feelings, including negative ones, by converting them into immediate action. In DoCoMo's first crisis, Ohboshi displayed this personality in spades. Instead of responding to the company's negativity and fear by lecturing about a malaise, or pondering its causes, he took to the road. Ohboshi lost no time in meeting with as many employees as possible. To dispel the ever-present cloud, he told them he had a five-year plan to make the fledgling, floundering DoCoMo a company they could all be proud of. "Trust me to do this," he told them, "I guarantee I can."

Bold words, likely to lift morale for a while. But how do you remake a company that has started from such a bad place? Ohboshi prided himself on being a pretty good marketer; he'd actually written books on marketing in the telecommunications industry. So he decided that he would draw on this area of his own professional strength and work to become the company's number one marketer.

Figure 3-2. NTT DoCoMo mobile phone sales: 1979–1994.

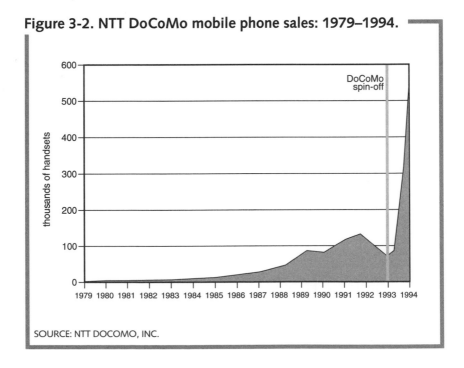

SOURCE: NTT DOCOMO, INC.

Naturally, he started fast and with any good marketer's first step: research.

Box 3-2. The lifetime employment system.

Everyone knows about Japan's vaunted lifetime employment system. In the West, though, only a few are aware of the two fairly deep problems with this common term:

- It is not a system.

- It is not for a lifetime.

And it never was.

There was a predisposition for the largest Japanese firms to hire employees fresh out of school and then try to keep them even through difficult economic times. Obviously, the high-growth 1960s and 1970s made the labor market somewhat tight and companies were eager to hold on to trained and loyal employees.

But even in its heyday, the lifetime employment system never applied to more than about 30 percent of Japan's working population. And since women were rarely, if ever, included in this category, the real percentage of the population represented was more like 15 percent.

Japan's economic woes through the 1990s have made this number even smaller. Although many top executives (in their fifties) still can claim to have been with one company for their entire career, it is harder and harder to find a thirty-something manager who hasn't changed jobs at least once.

Box 3-3. Naming the company.

Out of 3,000 suggested names for the new company, the list was narrowed to these three:

- Mobile Com

- Surcom

- DoCoMo

The new management team had to decide on the final name. The first two were ruled out because Mobile Com was "too simple" and "sounded like an oil company." The group also decided that Surcom really didn't leave any impression.

DoCoMo was a play on the Japanese phrase "doko demo" or "everywhere." Many of the employees thought that DoCoMo left too much of an impression, though. Some employees threatened not to answer the phone because they were ashamed of the new name. Hard to find any employees shrinking from the name these days…

A Little CEO Homework

Less than a year into his new job, he loaded up a box with every customer complaint form he could find. Picture this: the company's CEO, a senior executive with decades of experience and an entire company to draw on, carrying a cardboard box of complaint forms home for the night, then actually reading every one—700 in all—by himself. Crazy time management? No, just Ohboshi impatience. Obviously he could have assigned this work to others. But it would not have happened until the following day, at the earliest. And if it turned into a committee task, which would have been perfectly natural, DoCoMo might have taken a week to come to the same conclusions he would develop after one evening. Ohboshi simply didn't want to wait.

Impatience is more than a feeling for this chairman. He says that he believes the key to management is speed. It is clear that he's talking about a payoff measured in more than just time. On paper, even a week's delay would hardly have mattered. But there was hidden value, as there so often is, in reaching the point of *no delay at all*. One benefit of Ohboshi's impatience in this instance was that it drove him to do the complaint analysis himself. So the power of the CEO's rapid insight was applied to what was, after all, the company's most pressing problem. Equally important, having met the data himself, he could feel confident ownership of the problem.

The Three Big Complaints

As the CEO read through complaint forms, three themes quickly emerged. Placing the sheets into stacks according to the category of complaint, Ohboshi soon realized that most customer complaints centered around the following three topics:

1. Network issues

2. Handset issues

3. Price issues

A Network Made for Cars

The next day in the office, he took on these three categories in the order in which they had emerged. The network problems were easy to explain. Until the Motorola StarTAC phone had reached their market, Japanese had been reluctant to *carry* cell phones at all; they had simply been too big and bulky. So the vast majority of cellular phones sold until the early 1990s had been car phones. This, in turn, shaped the infrastructure. To facilitate a car phone network, you only need to install base stations along the busiest streets and major highways in the country. If you're using a car phone (versus a handheld), you may drive through a "dead area," but you'll be out of it soon. Most people are willing to put up with that level of inconvenience. But with handhelds, buyers aren't confined to streets—and they really want to use them everywhere.

Ohboshi saw this when the handheld market was just emerging and quickly realized that extra investment would be required to extend consistent service to all areas of Japan. Once the issue had been framed, every top executive realized that the investment simply could not be avoided; the new company simply couldn't afford these kinds of problems for its fledgling handheld services. If it became a common complaint that DoCoMo's StarTAC didn't work except where you used a car phone anyway, sales would drop even lower. It didn't take the spin-off team long to put all of the decisions in place to ensure that network complaints wouldn't plague them into the future.

Handsets That Didn't Quite Work

Returning to his complaint analysis, Ohboshi found that handset issues were a little more time-consuming. Although there were few complaints about the StarTAC equipment, the Japanese-made responses (even smaller and lighter phones) drew considerable fire from consumers. Ohboshi and his team worked on this one together. They ended up actually visiting the factories of NEC, Hitachi, Fujitsu, and Matsushita. After a set of discussions at Matsushita's Kakegawa factory, it was determined that the central issue was components: Manufacturers either were not receiving enough of the necessary components or were supplied with components that were too large for the new, smaller phones.

Handset manufacturers were doing their best to deal with the problem, but the factory floor "workarounds" were leading to quality problems. In true cockroach fashion, Ohboshi and his team scuttled directly to the offices of Toyo Tsushin, the supplier of the components, to sort things out. After a set of meetings, a rollout of new incentives, and a discussion of the importance of these components, the supplier agreed to the specs and volumes that DoCoMo's manufacturers required—and made good on delivery.

Start-up Costs As High As Mortgage Payments

The final complaint issue was money. And it really turned out to be two different problems. The first, startup costs, was born of DoCoMo's NTT heritage. At that time, a customer who wanted to have a home landline installed by NTT would pay about 70,000 yen—almost $650! The startup fee for a mobile phone was lower, but only by a little, at about 60,000 yen. But *on top* of that fee, the mobile subscriber had to put down a deposit to guarantee return of the 100,000 yen rental handset. This made the startup costs of getting a cellular phone much more expensive than getting a landline. With this pricing structure, a relatively wealthy person might add a mobile phone as a second line, but most of the market would not even consider getting a cell phone; it just cost too much.

Ohboshi knew that cellular phones could become DoCoMo's golden goose—but startup costs were threatening to kill this goose before it had a chance to lay any eggs. As he and his team considered the price barrier, they realized that the default NTT policy they had simply carried over to DoCoMo (requiring a deposit commensurate with the price of the telephone equipment) was a mistake in this new industry. It was expensive and, less obviously, it just wasn't necessary. After all, even if a cell phone was stolen, it couldn't work without going through DoCoMo's network. So the phone wasn't all that desirable a target and stood a pretty good chance of being recovered. And—here was the kicker—even if it *was* lost or stolen, customers would still pay a replacement fee, buying a new handset to retain the mobile service they had come to depend on. Tradition and habit said otherwise, but a hefty deposit was no longer necessary. With a short memo to the sales force, Ohboshi cut the startup costs of owning a cell phone in Japan by half.

Airtime Too Costly to Actually Use

The second money problem, connection costs, had less to do with DoCoMo's NTT origins and more to do with the industry's state of development. A patient person might even have said it wasn't a problem at all, just a phase to grow out of in time. Connection costs ("tariffs") in Japan were almost triple the costs in the United States. In essence, this just reflected different cost structures; about three times as many Americans were using cellular phones, so American providers, and users, enjoyed economies of scale. Ohboshi figured that when Japanese used cell phones as much as Americans, the rates would drop to about the same level. But given the nation's slow adoption of this particular technology, and other differences between the Japanese and U.S. mobile markets, it looked like an intractable chicken-and-egg problem. Japanese were staying away from cellular phones because service cost too much, but cellular service was never going to get cheaper with so few people subscribing. To an impatient Ohboshi, the solution seemed simple: Lower the connection costs to U.S. levels, betting that the number of users would quickly rise, thus making the service profitable even at the lower price.

It was an amazing stroke of courage, insight, and perhaps some luck. And it was another case where impatience paid off. Until that time, Japanese users had purchased only about 80,000 units per year, on average, for more than a decade. After DoCoMo's price cuts, handset sales rapidly shot to sixty times that level. From 1995 to the end of the millennium, Japanese customers bought more than 5 million DoCoMo phones per year.

CRISIS 2
The Case of the Plunging Market Share

No sooner had DoCoMo weathered the initial crisis—restoring healthy sales after that life-threatening slump—than another crisis emerged. This one came on with less drama. But, in the long run, it posed an equal threat. Although DoCoMo's financial results looked good overall, Ohboshi was concerned about weakening market share in Osaka and Nagoya. After a few months it was clear that the market share problem was spreading to other areas of Japan as well. Market share in Tokyo remained fairly strong, but how long could that last? And what was going wrong in the rest of the country?

Although Ohboshi's experience in NTT had trained him well in most issues of marketing and market research, there was one area that pre-1990s NTT could not have prepared him for. Like its model, AT&T of the 1970s and before, NTT throughout Ohboshi's years there was a monopoly. So actual competition—the driving force of life in most businesses—just wasn't a factor. (There were plenty of other challenges. As any career public servant can tell you, market competition isn't the only source of pressure in the world. It just feels that way to the rest of us.) Not surprisingly, DoCoMo's market share issue was all about competition.

It took a while for Ohboshi's team to understand the issues involved in the market share mystery. Why would market share be dropping outside Tokyo and not inside? What were the competitors doing differently?

The answer, it turned out, was an unforeseen result of DoCoMo's earlier stroke of genius—the one that opened up the market for mobiles by dropping the price. DoCoMo had originally adopted a strategy of targeting business people. That made so much sense, it was almost painful: Mobile service was expensive, business people were more likely than others to be able to afford cell phones, and they could more easily derive tangible value from mobility. By targeting this key population, DoCoMo could reduce selling and marketing expenses, focusing on the customer they most wanted. They could also improve service to these all-important business people.

But with the surge in the Japanese mobile market—a surge that DoCoMo had brought on—the environment changed. When DoCoMo lowered the handset deposits and connect charges on phones, their competitors followed suit. And the overall increase in sales of phones created economies of scale that brought handset prices down from about 40,000 yen to 10,000 yen. All of this combined to create an opportunity that DoCoMo's competitors saw before DoCoMo itself did: Lower prices meant that the businessperson was not necessarily the marketing "sweet spot" any more.

This was especially true for DoCoMo's competitors, who had never had the strong position with business customers that DoCoMo enjoyed. Pursuing less lucrative, but numerous, consumers, they expanded their distribution channels outside city centers into suburban areas. The lower prices meant that there were more consumers willing to buy, so they opened stores all over the country to service this broader need for cell phones.

DoCoMo's best move wasn't at all obvious. Sure, competitors were selling a lot of phones outside Tokyo. But the plain and simple fact was that the best customers, and the highest margins, were still right where DoCoMo had been targeting so successfully all along. Japan's (mainly urban) businesspeople were still spending more on cell phone services than the average consumer. Looking at the complex market share picture, Ohboshi realized that he wanted to match the expanding *service area* of his competitors without diluting the *level of service* he was able to give to his core customers—and all this while keeping prices low.

"One lesson I learned from all of this

was that what is most important about

management is speed."

—KOUJI OHBOSHI

The impatient Ohboshi chose a solution that was extremely fast to implement: Keep a small number of DoCoMo-owned stores in city centers, then outsource the rest. After one year of implementing the plan, DoCoMo actually owned just sixteen stores around the nation. But some 200 other DoCoMo shops were owned by others, mostly electronics manufacturers trying to sell handsets—Matsushita, NEC, Hitachi. Using the leverage and freedom provided by these partners, it took almost no time for DoCoMo to win back the market share dominance it had established early on.

The impatient executive is often mistaken for the hasty or impulsive one. And there is a common, almost automatic, assumption that fast solutions are less than the best. The phrase "quick and dirty" comes to mind. But Ohboshi's story demonstrates where both these beliefs go wrong. Embracing speed does not mean sacrificing quality. In this case, DoCoMo could have chosen a hasty solution, say, by expanding its company-owned stores from 16 to 200 during that same one-year period. But the quality of service to its key buyers might have been lost.

Rather than assuming that speed was more important than quality, Ohboshi focused his impatient demand on the right goal: a fast solution that still preserved DoCoMo's most important customer base. That demand forced the team to do some innovative thinking about distribution channels. The solution was still quick, but far from dirty; in the end, DoCoMo not only regained market share without alienating business users, but also cemented relationships with some of its key equipment suppliers by giving them a piece of the retail action.

FIGURE 3-3. DoCoMo mobile-phone market share net increase.

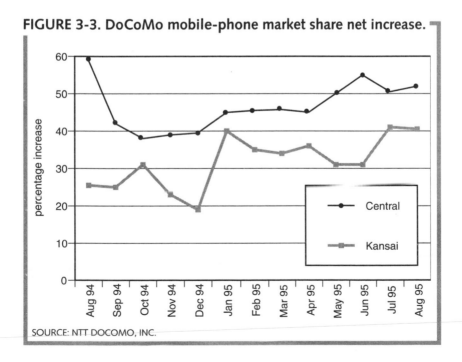

SOURCE: NTT DOCOMO, INC.

Box 3-4. DoCoMo subscriber growth.	
December 1979:	Launch
February 1993:	1 million
April 1996:	5 million
February 1997:	10 million
October 1997:	15 million
August 1998:	20 million
June 1999:	25 million
May 2000.	30 million
February 2001:	35 million
February 2002:	40 million

CRISIS 3
The Case of the Self-Actualized Consumer

It wasn't long before the impatient CEO was at it again. This time, though, the crisis wasn't thrust upon him. Neither did it sneak up on DoCoMo, as the market share issue had. Instead, this third crisis was created when Ohboshi impatiently looked ahead on the growth curve, saw the day it would flatten out—and began trying to find a solution.

By 1996, Ohboshi could see that the network was growing much more quickly than he'd anticipated. This was great for revenue growth, but it also meant that the market would saturate quickly. In the early days of DoCoMo, he had estimated an annual growth rate of 30 percent. That sounded aggressive—to his former colleagues in NTT, it may have sounded insane—but almost conceivable. And if the new company *could* hit that number, it would face a growing market for fifteen years. Plenty of time, then, to worry about saturation.

But as we know, DoCoMo's growth was *much* faster—about 100 percent annually. With the market doubling every year, Ohboshi estimated that it would only be about five more years before the firm hit 80 percent market penetration. And it would be tough to get much more than that.

Of course, growth in the number of users wasn't everything. After all, mobile phone operators are basically utilities. Once users embrace the telephones, they have to pay for the service year in and year out. So even with full market saturation, the business model is pretty sound. As long as you don't lose customers, you have an annuity. And if you can persuade customers to use more volume, or drive down your own costs, it is still possible to increase profits for quite some time. In this case, however, the competition in the Japanese market was driving annual revenue per user (ARPU) down. And with ARPU dropping relatively quickly, and growth sure to slow, DoCoMo was looking at three or four years of revenue growth. *Then* what?

Stopping Commoditization Quickly

Facing the revenue growth question brought an even bigger threat to light. Once you begin imagining the mature market, you become intensely concerned about protecting market share and whatever ability you have to charge premium prices. This is one of the places where impatience was most critical. At a time when business could not have looked better, Ohboshi's mind had scuttled ahead to the day that growth would slow. From there, it had caromed to the Really Big Question: How could DoCoMo continue differentiating itself from the competition—especially in ways that mattered to the buyer? Building on traditional NTT strengths, DoCoMo had done a great job of expanding its network and digitalizing service. This gave it a real technical edge over competitors—perhaps as much as a couple of years' worth.

The problem was that the people who really mattered didn't know or care about this edge. The battle for customers was not being waged on the technical front; it was a fight won or lost in large electronic stores around the country. When consumers in Akihabara or Shinjuku walked past a store like Yodobashi Camera or Big Camera, they were barraged by hundreds of types and colors of cell phones. In that context, getting them to focus their attention on the reliability of DoCoMo's network, or the advantages of digital service, would require a highly visible difference.

And that was just the beginning. As the cockroach president wandered out into the frenzy of consumer cell-phone buying circa 1996, he discovered even more threatening trends. To Ohboshi's shock, none of his DoCoMo phones were being displayed in the front of the store. The only companies with phones up front were the ones subsidizing their sales. In some cases, the subsidies were almost total; Ohboshi saw 30,000-yen phones being sold to consumers for 2 yen. When he returned to the office, he told his colleagues "this isn't price destruction any longer, this is price disappearance."

This was obviously a problem that required an innovative solution—or perhaps a more drastic approach. Ohboshi was, of course, more eager than anyone to find it, more impatient about getting to the solution quickly. But he demanded that it be more than a gut-level reaction. In such an extreme and unexplored environment, it was critical that DoCoMo understand the basic laws of the universe. What would economic principles—the equivalent of Newton's laws—predict for this world? Having studied law in school, Ohboshi had no formal training in economics. But he had read economics books as an avocation. Now he turned back to those readings to try to understand what to do with "price disappearance."

Basic economic theory didn't give him much hope. Once a product has become a commodity, there is almost no way to turn things around. That told Ohboshi that the only way to get out of this mess was to jump to an entirely new level of competion—to change the game, and fast. With that in mind, he continued scuttling through academic literature. He felt sure he would find the right model to help his team succeed in this strange new world. He considered some general economics theories that forecast the rise of the information economy—the importance of the material economy giving way to the immaterial. But in the end it was a classic theory from another wing of social science that really sparked his new thinking.

Thinking about the shift from a material economy to an information-based one, Ohboshi turned to Maslow's hierarchy of needs (see Box 3-5). Economic theory was telling him that society was about to move from a focus on material (which mapped roughly to "physiological" or "security" needs in Maslow's hierarchy) to a focus on information (which seemed more related to the cognitive, aesthetic, and self-actualization needs higher up Maslow's ladder). This shift, he decided, must be reflected in the products that his company was going to produce. Ohboshi had to move DoCoMo from concentrating on the physical to emphasizing the emotional.

Box 3-5. Maslow's hierarchy of needs.

1. **Physiological:** hunger, thirst, bodily comforts, etc.

2. **Safety/security:** out of danger

3. **Belonging and Love:** to affiliate with others, to be accepted

4. **Esteem:** to achieve, be competent, gain approval and recognition

5. **Cognitive:** to know, to understand, and to explore

6. **Aesthetic:** symmetry, order, and beauty

7. **Self-actualization:** to find self-fulfillment and realize one's potential

8. **Transcendence:** to help others find self-fulfillment and realize their potential

---

Making Them Emotional

For guidance, Ohboshi then looked to the "emotional" products already in the marketplace. How did the firms behind these products create value? As president of a major brand in Japan, he had long known that brand was important. But coming from an industry so based on technology and physical performance, he'd never really tried to consider the elements of brands in terms of emotions before. Once he had made this connection in his mind, he saw the evidence everywhere he looked.

Why were Japanese consumers willing to pay $500 for a Louis Vuitton bag when a $25 generic bag would fill the same function? Because of the emotional values attached to the brand Louis Vuitton. Here was proof that emotional content could be a big money maker. About the time that Ohboshi faced the challenge of keeping DoCoMo differentiated in a world of commodity bandwidth (1997), Moët Hennessy Louis Vuitton (LVMH) reported a 55 percent increase in sales in just six months.

"So I thought we have to shift the focus

from the material product to service, which

belongs to the pleasure industry."

—KOUJI OHBOSHI

Ohboshi was convinced that this shift from the physical to the emotional was an important idea to put into the company's strategy. This has proven prescient. As Patrick Lynch, one of our colleagues at the Accenture Institute for Strategic Change, found several years later, successful wireless data products worldwide are often those that somehow create an intimate, emotional bond with the user. Lynch's analysis is summarized in Appendix A.

For DoCoMo, Ohboshi saw, this strategy would have implications far beyond marketing. As he and his team started to envision what a new "emotional" marketplace for wireless communications would look like, they saw that there were some technical changes that would make the transmission of emotional content easier. One of these changes was the use of packet switching technology. Emotional content needed to be rich and instantaneous—there was almost no limit to the amount of bandwidth humans would value in supplementing or even replacing face-to-face experience.

Conceptually, it had been a long journey for Ohboshi on this third crisis, beginning with an eventual drop-off in revenue growth, and ending up at the need for packet-switched emotional content. Of course, it hadn't taken the cockroach president long to make these leaps. And, once there, he saw no reason to wait. In fact, he thought it would be easy to focus DoCoMo on this new challenge. He had only to share his vision of new technology supporting emotional products and services, and the thinking behind it, and the firm would take off in a burst of action, opening up a lead that no competitor could touch.

Trying to Get Executives to Hyperspeed

But for a huge number of players, the distance was too great, the speed too fast, and the process too flexible. Many in DoCoMo, from top executives on down, had come from NTT. Though working, and so far succeeding, in the hyperspeed world of information technology at the turn of the millennium, they were thoroughly steeped in their old systems. So key executives were not willing to buy into the new vision, at least not immediately. They thought that any new strategies for the company should be arrived at in a slow and methodical way. It was important to do all that *nemawashi* consensus building (see Box 3-6) before any decision could be made—no matter how strongly the president felt about a new idea. And this problem went far beyond the *torishimariyaku* (director) level.

But even if Ohboshi's direct reports had been willing to sign off on the strategy, he knew that the real struggle had to take place at lower levels in the organization. There, the problem would be not only accepting the vision, but conceding more concrete (seemingly trivial) battles. The technical people who worked on the regular cellular system didn't want to incorporate thinking from the new packet-switched network. They were reluctant—or at least slow—to implement this new packet-switched system because the difference in networks meant that engineers would have to completely relearn technical standards and practices. Ohboshi was asking people at every level of his organization to throw out their old expertise, become beginners again, and swallow their pride. Talk about emotional content!

And he was doing it at the worst possible time—the best times any company can experience. Though his attention had scuttled far into the future, in the day-to-day world, this was a period of tremendous growth and profitability for NTT DoCoMo. The company was having trouble keeping up with surging demand. So when word of Ohboshi's ideas for a new strategy started to get around, employees wondered about the president's state of mind. "Some people thought I had too much time on my hands, others figured I was getting old. There was speculation that I must have a rare blood type that was making me unpredictable and giving me stupid ideas."

"There was speculation that I must have a

rare blood type that was making me

unpredictable and giving me stupid ideas."

—KOUJI OHBOSHI

But the cockroach president was undeterred in his quest to build a new economy business that would be strong and profitable even after the party of initial adoption was over. He knew DoCoMo needed to act soon. He believed, as always, that following up the challenge right now, immediately, would reveal new opportunities and force creative solutions. And in any case, he was far too impatient to go through years of education and *nemawashi* before getting down to real work. So he did something unique in Japanese business history. On his own,

Ohboshi nailed his colors to the mast. Since he was president, it must be said, DoCoMo's colors were right up there with them.

Box 3-6. Nemawashi.

At its root (pun intended), the word *nemawashi* is a gardening term for preparing a tree for transplant. This involves digging around the tree and cutting some of its roots.

The word is used regularly in a business setting to mean "prior consultatation." In Japan, you are expected to give lots of notice of any kind of change or new idea and let people get used to the new concept over time. You do everything you can to make the "transplanted" idea take hold naturally. You never spring something new on your boss, your employees, or even your customers.

Putting It Out There

On July 19, 1996, Ohboshi paid for a full-page advertisement in the *Nihon Keizai Shinbun*, Japan's equivalent of the *Wall Street Journal*. In very small print, in an interview entitled "From Volume to Value," he laid out his vision for a new DoCoMo—as a commitment, not a possibility (see Appendix B).

Ohboshi followed this unprecedented public declaration of the corporation's vision with a "get together" for a select group: not his team at DoCoMo, and not the CEOs of DoCoMo's partners, but general managers (*bucho*) at DoCoMo's largest handset and technology suppliers. He knew that he needed buy-off and quick response to roll out this new set of technologies as quickly as possible. If he simply met with his fellow CEOs in these firms, the trickle-down time to key people in the companies would be months, if not years. But by laying out his vision for outsiders in a very public way, along with a schedule for rolling out this new strategy to the people who had to make that vision work, he saved valuable months that would have been lost to the bureaucratic processes so intrinsic to Japanese firms.

In trying to get a head start on his vision for DoCoMo's future, the chairman had gone around the system completely. We do not know of another example where the head of a major Japanese firm announced strategy in the press to force internal consensus. And the idea of meeting with middle-level managers in partner firms before asking for cooperation from the top first is downright un-Japanese. Even in the United States, it would raise eyebrows—and probably quite a bit more.

These initial moves alone were not enough. They required a whole effort, including action far beyond communications and PR. As one example, Ohboshi pushed hard to have i-mode—the flagship of this new emotional future—ready fast. He threatened to replace the i-mode team if it didn't have the product public by February 1999. Even in an authoritarian Japanese firm, threats like that simply are not made. The boss yells, people work harder, and the initial deadline is forgotten. And the threats certainly aren't held to. Mari Matsunaga, a key player in the i-mode team, complained that the president was trying to rush them too quickly. In an ordinary company, with ordinary leadership, the deadline would have been extended. But Ohboshi held firm.

And it worked. Less than three years later, i-mode made its debut—arguably the most successful technology introduction the world has ever known.

Learning from the Insect Kingdom?

The lessons of the cockroach president are classic, even basic. Yet...if we all know these lessons, why are they so rarely practiced, by CEOs, or by the rest of us? The overarching lesson, then, from the cockroach president, is the power of focusing on the basics and acting on them, instantly and intensely. Working within that principle, we might also emulate Ohboshi by remembering that:

■ *Leadership is hands on—even at the very top.* At every critical juncture, Ohboshi was there in person, getting his hands dirty: with the product (pushing for i-mode functionality), with the data (the details of market share), with production problems (the internal workaround), with customers (carrying home the cardboard box of complaint forms), and with the future (seeing emotion as the company's strategic advantage).

■ *Speed really can kill.* We have followed Ohboshi's story after he had been named the first CEO of DoCoMo, a company that happens to have created wealth on a world-class scale. But while learning from his success, we should also remember why he was given this opportunity: because he was *not* in line for the highest levels of the company he had served for so many years. The traits that opened this door for him, especially his impatience, almost certainly closed other doors along the way. So if the DoCoMo spin-off had not come along, things might have been very different. With slightly altered breaks, Ohboshi might never have been given the latitude to make his vision a reality. None of us would ever have heard of him, or perhaps of i-mode itself.

■ *But speed also creates—bigger and more often.* Chairman Ohboshi, of course, has not only thought deeply about speed; he has run a huge, uncontrolled experiment on its value: his own career. Looking back, he feels strongly that the opportunities created by impatience, over time, far outweighed its costs. From our point of view, looking at the results, it would be hard to disagree.

■ *Know when, and how, to bend the rules—or even break them.* Ohboshi's end run to launch i-mode—the newspaper ad, the manager meetings—was a bold play, but also carefully timed. It vividly illustrates the power of impatience. But the very way it stands out, even in the impatient Ohboshi's career, confirms that it was a dangerous play. Even the cockroach leader only dared do it once.

■ *In the end, focus on customers.* None of Ohboshi's impatience would have paid off if it had not been backed by his relentless focus on the central issue: delivering value to the customer. In every case we can think of, he found his way to the heart of the problem by thinking about what DoCoMo had to do, to win the customer's continued trade, affection, and respect—to give even more than was required.

CHAPTER FOUR

Luck

"We must believe in luck. For how else can we
explain the success of those we don't like?"
—JEAN COCTEAU

IF YOU LISTEN CAREFULLY to key executives in DoCoMo, you begin
to hear something really surprising. In the rational, competitive world of
twenty-first-century business, where the inexorable physics of "market
forces" self-consciously drives every decision; in the hard-edged, quantitative arena of telecomm, where relentless scientific advance is used to
deliver ever more digital bandwidth at ever less cost; in the orderly and
industrious island of modern Japan, where precision, consistency, and
hard work are the resources that really count—one of the strongest feelings associated with DoCoMo's success is, of all things, luck.

That lucky feeling hovering back there behind these wireless winners is not a small thing or a social convention. It is not the Japanese
business version of a quarterback's postgame interview—"aw, shucks,
we played our best and got a few breaks." No, what these guys are
thinking about, after all their hard work, sacrifice, and intelligence, is
absolute luck: unearned, unpredictable, completely uneven in size,
direction, and timing. This is stuff so...*random* that it would make
anybody nervous. You can't plan around it, you certainly can't take
credit for it, and there's no guarantee you'll ever see it again. So not

everybody will acknowledge it. But it's not hard to detect a profound belief that luck was really vital. You sense the strength of their conviction that those particular breaks and identifiable factors (which could easily have gone the other way) made all the difference.

And it's not just *inside* DoCoMo that people are thinking about luck, either. The first few years of the wireless economy have been, in the words of that famous Chinese curse, "interesting times." The technology has been more solid, and advanced more quickly, than anyone had a right to expect. The business models have seemed sensible. And, on paper, the environment couldn't be better for the advantages that mobile data provides. Yet full adoption (real, profitable use) has been spotty at best, disappointing almost everywhere. *Everywhere*, in fact… except where i-mode was launched.

So it's little wonder that some people believe DoCoMo was just plain lucky. These skeptics will tell you, softly perhaps, that there is no difference in performance that should make this one particular company any more successful than AT&T Wireless, Telia, Orange, or a half dozen other wireless data contenders worldwide. A lot more people, including potential competitors on three continents, hope those skeptics are right. Because the corollary would be that—despite DoCoMo's new size, despite its unparalleled success, despite its low-key but ominous moves to explore U.S. and European markets—the rest of the world has nothing special to fear. Sure, there's still the problem of getting wireless data to really take off, but that's nothing new.

We disagree.

That is, we believe that DoCoMo was lucky. But we also believe, with the late novelist Robertson Davies, that "what we call luck is the inner man externalized. We make things happen to us." That's why we classify luck as a feeling. The point Davies made so well, which strategists have been making for literally thousands of years, is this: Luck is not mainly a characteristic of events, but of people. Luck is an emotion, a mindset really, that we somehow project into the world. There are at least two ways to think about that. A lot of smart, sensible people believe that this feeling essentially causes lucky (or unlucky) events to occur. Many others won't go quite that far. But they will gladly acknowledge that, even on the purely concrete level, people's feelings have an awful lot to do with whether or not they consistently exploit whatever luck happens to them. However *you* think about this, the end result is the same. People, based at least partly on their internal emotions, "make their own luck."

Companies make their own luck, too. DoCoMo certainly did. Perhaps key people, or the culture itself, projected luck into a changeable universe. On the other hand, perhaps key people, or the culture itself, just had the right feelings to quickly see and exploit the lucky breaks that would have happened in any case. Either way, DoCoMo showed the world, not a textbook case of well-planned industrial blastoff, but the dream version, an investor's purest fantasy: the sudden, near-vertical rise from ho-hum spin-off to the most valuable company in all of Japan, and one of the most valuable in the world. Wherever luck comes from, with a little less of it, that trajectory might have been very different. The company would still have gone up, but would it have hit escape velocity? Even then, would it have reached its current altitude—a spot so far out there that some competitors, whose own efforts are still trapped in Earth's gravitational field, have to wonder: Is it time to scrub this mission entirely?

When you start thinking about those decisions, of course, the question of companies making their own luck suddenly gets much more serious. If you find yourself in the same part of the solar system as the still-soaring DoCoMo, if you'd like to invest, riding along as DoCoMo attempts to boldly go where no telecomm has gone before, or if you're planning a launch of your own and just want to emulate their success, then you need to know—*how lucky did DoCoMo get?* And *how did DoCoMo get lucky?* Only that will let you decide whether they are really that much better than everyone else (a formidable competitor, an ideal model) or simply a stray data point (something you can ignore on your own mission).

Of course, that's a big question. Luck boosted DoCoMo's trajectory at so many different points, in so many different ways, it would be impossible to even find them all, much less run the "what if" calculations. But you don't need to analyze *all* their luck. That's the beauty of such a dramatic success: The little things counted, but a few big things, things you can find without running regressions, really made the difference. To understand DoCoMo's luck, everything you need to know comes down to one central question: Why did i-mode take off so fast and so well? And the answer lies largely in just a few events. Understand those, and you'll understand how much to fear, or respect, DoCoMo. (You might even learn to make your own luck.)

That story begins with a single man, Keiichi Enoki. Luck aside, Enoki is important because he is the one person who, more than any other, injected entrepreneurial fire into i-mode. And it was the i-mode flame, of course, that ignited DoCoMo's huge second-stage acceleration, putting it way out there beyond any current competition. As we'll see, Enoki himself proved to be a very lucky man. But the greater luck may be that DoCoMo stumbled on him in the first place.

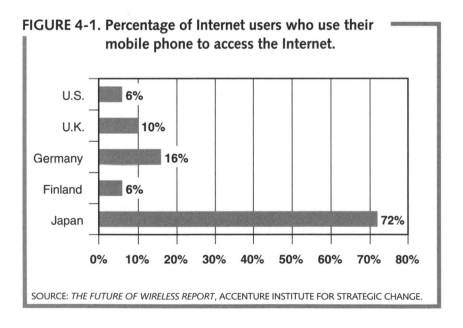

FIGURE 4-1. Percentage of Internet users who use their mobile phone to access the Internet.

SOURCE: *THE FUTURE OF WIRELESS REPORT,* ACCENTURE INSTITUTE FOR STRATEGIC CHANGE.

> ## Box 4-1. Luck: Regressions make it official.
>
> The first time John realized that life is really about luck, he was already in college. (How does one get so far before realizing that maybe one's lot in life isn't completely determined by hard work and talent? John is sure his mother had something to do with it.) It wasn't until he read Christopher Jencks' book *Inequality*[1] that he began to see the hand of fate everywhere.
>
> *Inequality* was written by Jencks and seven coauthors from the Center for Educational Policy Research at Harvard. When it was published, way back in 1972, *Newsweek* hailed it as "the most significant educational book of the year," and *The Christian Science Monitor* expected the work to "influence American educational policies for years to come." John read it first in a freshman sociology course. He hasn't seen it improve education much, but he learned an important lesson for business.
>
> In this research, eight of the most important educational researchers in the country, with all of the data resources imaginable at their time, tried to explain why people are not equal in income. Their conclusion was that "many popular explanations of economic inequality are largely wrong." Difference in individual outcomes couldn't be explained away by genetic differences, by the "fact that parents pass along their disadvantages to their children," or by "differences between schools" (p. 8).
>
> In fact, when they compared men (why would they include women in such a study in the 1970s, after all?) who were identical in family background, cognitive skill, educational attainment,

and occupational status, Jencks and the team found "only 12 to 15 percent less inequality than among random individuals" (p. 226). In other words, when you find yourself in company that might naturally be congratulated for its skill, fortitude, and hard work…it's not a bad thing to remember the role that luck played in getting you all there—and to remember that there are others, who have displayed equal skill, fortitude, and hard work, who just didn't make it.

It's nice to have statistics to remind us of this, of course. But surely, when we look at our own experience, didn't we already know? Anyone who has been to a "highly selective college" or who worked in one of those resume-making companies has met amazingly talented people, from all kinds of backgrounds. They have also met a surprising number of people who, as far as anyone can see, are no more exceptional than people at less celebrated institutions. The difference boils down to luck: having the right parents, perhaps, or the seemingly wrong ones; the serendipity of having that great teacher who somehow excited your interest in math; or the airline scheduling algorithm that somehow put you right next to the headhunter on the day she had the perfect job for you.

The authors concluded that "those who are lucky tend, of course, to impute their success to skill….In general, we think luck has far more influence on income than successful people admit" (p. 227). All the more reason, we believe, to get serious about making your own luck.

People, People Who Need People

Because luck has a lot to do with feelings and reactions—with people, not just events—the choice of people is absolutely critical. To be lucky in business, you need executives and managers and workers who will recognize, or attract, or exploit, good luck. DoCoMo faced the particular challenge of getting people who could do that in the rigorous environment of a startup...even though the entire original team came from an emphatically nonstartup background. The way they met that challenge—the way Ohboshi brought Enoki to DoCoMo and supported him—created a huge degree of DoCoMo's luck.

Why single out Enoki? After all, like any company that survives for long, DoCoMo has had good luck (the conventional, "aw shucks" kind) in the quality of founders and key executives who gravitated there. At the party, when it first becomes clear that the infant firm is going to survive into something approaching adolescence, it's customary to observe that without a team of visionary, energetic, ambitious risk-takers—extraordinary people—the enterprise would never have gotten off the ground. And in DoCoMo's case, that's absolutely, emphatically correct. The firm *was* created and led by very special people.

But that's not exactly luck. After all, what do any of us mean when we talk about a lucky break? We mean a good outcome that happens even though the odds were against it: something the smart money couldn't have bet on. And while the odds were against any *particular* member of the initial team being there—an impatient and unconventional Ohboshi, or a Tachikawa driven by a sense of inequality so deep that he will never, ever stop—the fact that DoCoMo began with extraordinary leaders is no surprise at all.

Think of it this way: Would the smart money ever bet that a large and prestigious corporation like NTT *couldn't* assemble a credible, talented team to lead the DoCoMo spin-off? As anyone knows who has worked in or competed against a large corporation, big companies are awash in talent. And no matter what the corporate culture, some minority of each company's talented high achievers will be eager for the challenge of a less rigid, more risky environment. Some will even be so rebellious or misplaced that they already have most of the skills and attitudes and instincts that it takes to turn a good idea into a successful business—even though these traits aren't typically rewarded in a large, established concern.

So for NTT to start DoCoMo with a great team is hardly a random event. But that alone would not have been enough. The history of spin-offs and entrepreneurial ventures from big organizations is littered with credible, talented teams that just didn't make it. And lots of those failed missions can be traced to the culture of established companies (see Box 4-2). The difference between that experience and what you need in a startup is huge. Many people who thrive in a big corporate environment can't change their traits and fit into startup mode at all. Others can adapt. But in our experience, they can't usually do it alone. They often need the right leader, mentor, or environment, some kind of catalyst showing them how to make the change they have dreamed of—maybe even forcing them to take the leap they think they want. They need to be willing to learn, but they also need something or someone to learn from. Sending them off to invent and live that culture on their own is very risky indeed. Coming from such a different world, they just don't have the right mindset.

The DoCoMo team was an example. Despite extraordinary strengths, traits that would prove crucial in the firm's success, the core team that ensured DoCoMo's immediate survival lacked the kind of experience it usually takes to create a startup mindset. And make no mistake: For i-mode to fly, a startup mindset was absolutely required. The elite NTT insiders who were initially spun off to lead the DoCoMo team did a great job supercharging the cellular phone business, which could easily have floundered. But that was a business everyone, including consumers, mainly understood. Mobile data—the niche where i-mode propelled DoCoMo so far beyond earthbound competitors—was a true, thin-air startup. No one could be positive that there was a business there at all. Even if it was *there*, no one could know exactly what it *was*.

Box 4-2. Is it paranoia if they're after you?

Insiders and investors often complain that big firms are too slow and cautious; they act fearful. It's easy to criticize these timid giants. What we often forget, though, is that these companies genuinely have something to fear.

Startups have nothing to lose. That's a matter of definition, but it's also a matter of faith. Many successful entrepreneurs, and probably more successful startup investors, argue that, if you have any way to achieve success without making the new company succeed, then you inevitably start hedging. And that, they say, is catastrophic because creating new things simply requires full-out effort. So all of us who benefit from innovation want entrepreneurs who believe their only course—their only survival—depends on making the new venture succeed.

That may be right for startups, but for big companies, it's crazy. They do have something to lose—lots of things. There's damaging the brand, creating legal problems, cannibalizing existing business, alienating partners, violating sensible HR policies, etc. And the humbling truth for "intrapreneurs" is that very few new products are important enough to outweigh those other things. The enterprise needs balance—the kind of project leader who can achieve operational goals without risking those community assets. The go-for-broke entrepreneur may be a folk hero, but he's seldom a good corporate citizen.

Lucky to Have Enoki

And that's where luck, in the form of Keiichi Enoki, really came in. He was in no way superior to DoCoMo's founding leadership—no more visionary, no more energetic, no more ambitious, not even necessarily more of a risk-taker. Yet Enoki was unique, and uniquely valuable, precisely because he *wasn't* a successful corporate guy. DoCoMo's top managers were, after all, drawn from the elite of NTT. They could not have risen without a healthy dose of the traits NTT valued most. Maybe they fit the standard profile less comfortably than their peers (who had ended up running NTT itself). But, at heart, they were all people who could have succeeded for a lifetime inside that highly bureaucratic monopoly. Enoki, on the other hand, was the kind of person who should not have been there at all. As the statisticians would say, he was an "outlier"—more than two standard deviations away from the NTT ideal. Or to put it in less quantitative terms, Enoki was "out there" (even compared to the DoCoMo's crew of executive renegades).

It was DoCoMo's great luck that Enoki had slipped through the filters into NTT, eluded the forces that reject unfamiliar types, and stayed out of trouble long enough to be there for DoCoMo to recruit. And it was good luck that the elite corporate figure guiding DoCoMo, Ohboshi, recognized Enoki's gift and gave him the freedom he needed. For Enoki turned out to be the random variation that could help DoCoMo's mindset evolve beyond the world of its parent. He had exactly the rare personality and outlook needed to help this extraordinary team do what it so much wanted to—but what its corporate experience, instincts, and training all worked so hard against.

A budding thespian in college, Enoki appeared in a variety of parts and plays in the drama club at Waseda University. That sounds conventional—until you really think about it. If you, personally, had a major investment to make, one involving real money and real risk of failure, would you turn to an *actor* to manage it? Even in the fame-worshipping and individualistic United States—even in Southern California—actors are seen as a little weird. After all, these are people who choose to stand on stage in front of other people (when surveys repeatedly tell us that more people fear speaking in public than fear death), who replace their own feelings and characteristics with ones that fit completely different people, and who spend a lot of time probing and displaying their emotions. We Americans don't mind a little charisma in our executives, but acting would be, well, over the top (except for the occasional chief executive of the nation). Now move this whole discussion to Japan. Sure, this is the culture that has supported centuries of Noh drama. But much more fundamentally it is the place where children learn that "the nail that stands out gets hammered down." In the kind of business environment that rises from a culture like that, where do actors fit in? Exactly; they don't.

Not quite fitting in, though, is what Enoki brought to i-mode. He has many of the traits needed for respectable success in any Japanese corporation; gifted in math, for example, he originally set out to become an engineer. But his personality has never quite been mainstream. Likewise, he joined a blue-chip Japanese corporation, NTT; but no one thought for long that this was a typical salaryman. He has far too much appetite for independence. "Throughout my career, I have always wanted to work for someone who would not monopolize things. I wanted the freedom to be creative." Not such a radical statement, perhaps—but try extracting it from a thousand successful employees of any Japanese corporation. And the need for independence, of course, is perhaps the single trait linking virtually every successful entrepreneur. By NTT standards, Enoki was quite the lone ranger. Yet he fell just a little short of the traditional entrepreneur's (fairly extreme) standard.

Enoki himself admits that he has never been quite able to kick the salaryman habit. "To go off and do something by myself....I don't have the entrepreneurial spirit to that extent." One of his key hires (not surprisingly, the most obviously unconventional figure in i-mode history), Mari Matsunaga, who played a key role under Enoki in developing i-mode, put it well, dubbing him a "super salaryman." In other words, Enoki represented a kind of a missing link between the entrepreneurs that DoCoMo needed and the rebellious corporate employees that it started with. For DoCoMo, this was the perfect mix,

Box 4-3. Why entrepreneurs don't fit most places.

Read the history of great companies, and you'll see the founders facing obstacles that are tougher, more numerous, longer lasting more surprising than they could ever have expected. But they keep going—probably even the unsuccessful ones—because that is who entrepreneurs are. As Nancy Koehn says in *Brand New*, her fine history of great brands from Wedgwood to Starbucks, entrepreneurs are the people who do whatever is necessary to bring the new idea to life.[2]

Think about what that really means. *Whatever is necessary*. Even laying off people you sought out, hired, and worked alongside? Sacrificing the friendship that brought your business to life in the first place? Investing every dollar you have and all you can borrow from the "friends, families, and fools"? Ask around Silicon Valley; those risks are absolutely taken for granted.

Whatever is necessary? A lawyer might say, "no business is worth breaking the law for." A psychologist, "ignoring your family just to get rich—that's crazy!" A financial planner, "never bet it all on one business, even your own." And, if we are honest, most of us agree. We can handle lottery tickets, visiting casinos, buying on margin, even getting married or having kids. But almost no one is willing to bet everything on any one thing, because we know that's nuts.

That's what separates most of us from entrepreneurs. They don't exactly fail to see these risks—though many we've met are good at denial; mainly, they just ignore them. Whatever is necessary. It's like the old joke: In a ham and egg breakfast, the chicken is involved; the pig is committed. Entrepreneurs, of course, are committed. Not surprisingly, that scares the rest of us, who are, basically…chickens.

maybe even the only mix that could have worked. Enoki was close enough to the NTT ideal to be there in the first place, without scaring off DoCoMo's top leadership (much less the NTT officials who approved his move into DoCoMo). But he was also close enough to the stereotype of a serial entrepreneur to make the series of intuitive management leaps that it always seems to take to create a truly innovative product—and the business that surrounds it.

Enoki's luck (at surviving as an essentially foreign element inside NTT) and DoCoMo's luck (at having him) began long before DoCoMo itself. "For the most part, I was fortunate to have pretty good bosses on my way up in the organization," he says. Ohboshi turned out to be the best possible match. "After outlining the basic idea of data over phones, he put me in charge and set me free." Enoki emphasizes how lucky he and his team were to have a top executive who was willing to leave a development team alone. Instead of defending their plans and second-guessing corporate priorities, the team was able to actually develop i-mode.

That luck, and the Enoki-catalyzed independence, was visible right away. The first question i-mode had to face was what "the mobile data market" would really be. Everyone agreed that wireless data would be a big market, someday. Chairman Ohboshi was bolder and more specific; he had become convinced that data service on mobile phones was the next big thing. But exactly what service would *start* this next big thing? The young company, like huge competitors still working in the United States and Europe, had to go from the promise of a great technology to the harsh and impatient market challenge of a startup: What applications of mobile data could be successfully sold *right now*? The smart money wasn't betting on ringtones and screensavers. An important consulting report that

DoCoMo commissioned during this time suggested that data services would be most profitable in the interactive personal digital assistant (PDA) arena. Researchers were duly assigned to start playing around with ways to get PDAs to interact with their phones so that their customers carrying both a phone and a PDA could interface with their home or office computer and get important information downloaded to their Palm or other device. It seemed like a reasonable idea. It was certainly being promoted elsewhere.

But, luckily, the man assigned to start the digital services operations (Enoki) wasn't convinced that PDAs were the way to go. And even more luckily—even less predictably—his boss, Chairman Ohboshi, did not force him to prove he was right before moving forward. In the face of an unknown and at that point truly unknowable market, he let the in-house entrepreneur follow his instincts.

Box 4-4. Culture club.

Even with the real risks they face, it seems large firms should innovate more. After all, they have money, people, contacts, information, and know-how that startups can only dream of. They're big enough to survive mistakes. And they must have done something right, probably including innovation, to get where they are.

Ah, but they also have that factor we hear so much about, "entrenched corporate culture." But what do people mean by that? They mean a natural and quite powerful set of human feelings, driven by the reality of not being a startup.

Like any organization that has survived for long in a harsh environment, big companies develop fairly strong cultures—they have to. Those cultures, partly for "rational" economic reasons and partly for motives that are merely human, tend to reject anyone who doesn't fit their profile. And for most established cultures, strong entrepreneurial behavior is ample cause for rejection.

A startup is like a small group of soldiers behind enemy lines. The people inside the group won't literally die if the mission fails, but on some level they believe they will. They can certainly act that way. In a startup, as on the battlefront, the soldiers all come from different places, for different reasons, and have real lives that will last longer and must be more important. Yet for the duration they all act as if this is the most important thing in life. It doesn't make sense, but it seems to work emotionally. And emotions are what it takes to take that kind of risk.

An established company isn't in a short-term survival situation. Whatever any one person does, the community will be there after every current member is gone. That changes the game. People may still work hard and take risks. But the group unconsciously rejects that kind of battlefield commitment; it's too dangerous. The community tends to value stable, predictable behavior—actions it can understand and therefore plan around. Hedging, collaborating, avoiding losses and negative attention—all these become much more important. Heroes are fine, but they need to be sensible and predictable.

To put it in baseball terms, what this stable community wants is a nice string of solid singles and a reasonable batting average. They like home run hitters, sure, but all those strikeouts make them nervous.

Free Your Team; Success Will Follow

Creating this unconventional team was, in a word, critical. Because when he was assigned by the president of DoCoMo to create what became i-mode, Keiichi Enoki was a team of one. In fact, he was told that because DoCoMo itself was so small at the time, he would be the only current employee assigned to the project team; if Enoki needed people to work on the project, he would have to find them outside DoCoMo. After some unsuccessful experiences with headhunters, Enoki began calling his own contacts to ask for their advice.

One of his first calls was to Masafumi Hashimoto, an old friend with a gift. Hashimoto ran a printing company, Sun Color, in Kumamoto, Japan. Kumamoto is a beautiful city wedged between the mountains and the sea on the southern island of Kyushu. Not a major posting, but still a relatively important city because of the high-tech industry that has grown up there. When NTT had stationed Enoki in Kumamoto in the early 1990s, he had befriended Hashimoto. They became regular drinking buddies and had stayed in touch with each other ever since.

Hashimoto prided himself on entrepreneurship. And as head of a much smaller firm than NTT, he had faced the opportunity—in fact, the pressing need—to learn skills that aren't often valued in a large corporate environment. His gift, the one Enoki hoped to call on, was a special skill at helping creative young people find a niche for themselves in his company, or in companies around the country. Enoki called Hashimoto, in part, because he knew that creativity was probably what was most required in developing this undefined new business of wireless data. And when Enoki turned to his friend for ideas about starting a strong, innovative team at DoCoMo, Hashimoto knew how to find the right people. The first name on his lips was Mari Matsunaga.

Matsunaga's background was even less traditional than Enoki's. As Japan was bursting from the prosperous 1980s into the volatile 1990s, she served as an executive in one of the nation's most revolutionary firms, Recruit. She then climbed to become the managing editor of one of the country's most popular magazines, *Travaille*. And in the process

---

Box 4-5. It's not easy being queen.

It was from Kouji Ohboshi that Enoki learned one of his favorite terms: noblesse oblige. "The reason Britons are willing to put up with their upper class," the younger man explains, "is that the aristocrats know their obligation to society. In both World War I and World War II, there was a higher death rate among the upper crust than in the lower ranks. This shows their understanding of their position and obligation to preserve the freedom and happiness of the rest of the society. That's noblesse oblige," he says.

When, in the crucial early moments of i-mode's conception, Ohboshi gave Enoki support and protection from typical bureaucratic oversight, that was a powerful lesson in noblesse oblige. Having felt its value for himself, Enoki decided that he needed to do the same thing for any team that he brought on board. Moving forward with this attitude, blending Ohboshi's leadership with his own unconventional instincts, Enoki was able to attract people that NTT, for instance, would never have hired. That enabled him to create the mix of people that would make i-mode a reality.

Matsunaga became something of a celebrity. She would eventually even land a seat on Japan's prestigious National Tax Commission.

When You're on a Roll

NTT—or even an NTT spin-off—is not the kind of place most would expect Mari Matsunaga to migrate. But Enoki saw the fit. Matsunaga, too, seemed to instinctively recognize the creative potential. She did insist (and Enoki, demonstrating his own noblesse oblige, ensured) that she be allowed to hire some people of her choosing. The first one that she brought in was Takeshi Natsuno. She had met Natsuno when he worked part time at Recruit when he was a college student. Another innovator with an eclectic background, Natsuno was definitely not the type to survive long in any single firm, at least not in a conventional one. But his talent had taken him lots of places. Natsuno had worked for Tokyo Gas, earned an M.B.A. from a U.S. school, joined an American consulting firm, and finally decided to become an Internet entrepreneur.

Box 4-6. Recruit Co., Ltd.

Recruit had started as a publishing firm, putting out an employment guide for newly graduating students in the 1960s. During Japan's go-go years (the 1980s and early 1990s), it was one of the fastest growing companies in the country. It boasted buildings all over Tokyo, top executives who hobnobbed with the most powerful politicians in Japan, and impressive real estate holdings. Exactly because of all the hobnobbing, the popularity of the firm waned because of political scandal, but it is still a very viable firm with more than seventy-five weekly and monthly publications.

For i-mode, Natsuno's particular gift was to grasp the creative concepts that Mari described and translate them into business plans that would capture the attention of sophisticated venture capitalists. He was also a real salesman, known for stopping just short of exaggeration when he described i-mode's potential. It takes a special gift to always paint the most compelling picture imaginable of an unknown technology, particularly in the early stages when the details and even the major elements of the picture—the capabilities, demand, and business model—are changing almost daily. If Enoki, through his friends and non-NTT hires, had not reached outside the corporate world, he might never have found that gift for i-mode.

Creative recruiting in the world beyond NTT was obviously vital. But not all the innovation came from outside. Enoki found surprising resources inside DoCoMo, as well. After he recruited Matsunaga—despite the original warnings—he was able to bring over five young employees from DoCoMo. One of these was Takao Sasakawa. A gung-ho player from a very wealthy family, Sasakawa, too, injected more energy and innovation than anyone could have expected. When the i-mode team was trying to impress the Zagats

---

"Luck is of little moment to the great

general, for it is under the control of

his intellect and his judgment."

—LIVY

(of the *Zagat Guides*—one of their first non-Japanese content plays), the chosen meeting location was Sasakawa's spacious, almost unimaginably rare family home. (Of course, the Japanese had to spend much of the time there reassuring the Zagats that this was *not* the level of accommodation typical travelers to Japan should expect.)

Matsunaga also describes as typical the time when, early in the process of thinking about companies who might work with DoCoMo to provide i-mode content, Sasakawa suggested that he knew someone at Oriental Land, the company that runs Disneyland in Japan. Without much discussion, Sasakawa set up a meeting with his acquaintance. It was only just before the meeting that anyone realized that Sasakawa's friend just happened to be the *president* of this potentially huge partner.

Knowing these inside stories, it's not hard to see someone like Takao Sasakawa—or Mari Matsunaga, who found him; or Masafumi

Hashimoto, who found *her;* or Keiichi Enoki, who hired them all—as a lucky break. Looking at results, too, it's tempting to see the entire i-mode effort as incredibly lucky. Starting with no clear vision of product or even market demand, DoCoMo created i-mode, a product that in just three years would be used by 30 million people. That's faster growth than any dot-com we're aware of. And those are paying subscribers, so i-mode was well in the black. (At a comparable moment in its history, the typical dot-com was a bonfire of VC cash—the hotter the better.) And they did all that with Enoki's team of just fifty people.

Is It Better to Be Lucky Than Good?

So in what is arguably the single most important dimension of creating a new business—building the right team—DoCoMo had some incredible bits of luck. Does that make the company's success nothing more than a fluke? A surprising number of people, including once and future competitors, would like to think so. Some are even acting on that assumption. They are not pushing hard to understand what has made i-mode so successful. They are not translating DoCoMo tactics into American or European contexts. They are not preparing themselves adequately to compete against the new giant. And by making these decisions—by banking on the idea that DoCoMo just got lucky—they are themselves taking an enormous chance.

Of course, the "lucky break" assumption is not a crazy one. Especially with i-mode, DoCoMo has caught some breaks, far beyond somehow finding the exact, rare people who could successfully create an innovative and nimble startup in the shadow of a lumbering monopoly. Beginning with that observation, some would argue that introducing wireless data to consumers was a kind of worldwide lottery. Someone, somewhere, would eventually win the big jackpot. It just happened to be in Japan, and i-mode just happened to win. Others, though, see a totally different picture. Mindful of the coaches' maxim "luck is the residue of hard work," they say that the critical factor is not what breaks fall your way, but rather what you do with them.

We don't presume to answer this question scientifically. We're not even sure it is answerable, in a final and objective way, for i-mode or for anyone. But every manager, every executive, every investor, even (in this era of free agency) every employee ends up coming to some answer for themselves. They have to, because that answer, recognized or not, guides their behavior as they try to create or exploit lucky breaks of their own—and deal with the luck that befalls their competitors.

For ourselves, we believe that much more than random good fortune has been at work. Finding the right people is crucial, and DoCoMo had some luck there. But key people also made some very smart, deliberate decisions—starting at least as far back as hiring Enoki—which created a kind of chain reaction. Good decisions, good people, and the resulting good luck have compounded, with Enoki turning to Hashimoto, who recommended Matsunaga, who brought in Sasakawa and Natsuno. As we will see, the energy bouncing around among these people created not just a new product, but a radical new creative culture.

In sum, *DoCoMo successfully transformed itself into the kind of organization that makes its own luck.* You can see this chain reaction at work—actually see the luck being created—by examining five of DoCoMo's luckiest breaks. Each one, at first, seems to have nothing to do with what happened inside DoCoMo. And each one, in the end, reveals the power of building a lucky team.

1. *DoCoMo was lucky that the Internet hadn't taken off yet in Japan.* In 1993, almost no one except university researchers and computer scientists had even heard of the Internet. By 2000, almost 50 percent of Americans were using it. In that same year, though, only 15 percent of Japanese had Internet access. Why was this equally affluent and arguably more technology-loving population so slow to embrace the net? Many theories have been floated: That because Japanese homes are so small, consumers weren't willing to invest the space a computer requires; that Japanese offices are too cramped for a computer on every desk; that Japanese kanji are too difficult to input from a keyboard; or that Japanese telecomm charges are so high that con-

necting was prohibitive. Of course, Japanese homes and offices are still small, kanji are still tough to type, and phone rates there are still outrageous by our Western standards. Yet the Internet (fixed as well as mobile) has now taken off in Japan, leaving these common theories far behind. What we know is that, among the affluent nations of the world, Japan was extremely slow in Internet takeup, a real outlier. The reason remains a mystery.

What is not a mystery is how this worked to DoCoMo's advantage. Soon after she was hired, Enoki's i-mode manager, Mari Matsunaga, argued that the best source of data for a mobile device could be found in the Web sites already being developed both in Japan and outside of Japan. At the time, this seemed radical. People in Japan weren't using the Net at all; why would they use an expensive, limited bandwidth version on their cell phones? Why not, instead, the classic low-bandwidth/high-value application: the PDA?

Matsunaga knew why not. She understood that most Japanese had not computerized their own personal information, even after many generations of competent portable devices. Adding wireless data would make those devices even more powerful and convenient, but her intuition was that a PDA solution would still not interest many Japanese users. So she rejected the conventional wisdom that PDA solutions would drive the market for wireless data. At the same time, she knew that many companies were in the process of getting rudimentary Web sites established in Japan. She thought that much of this simple, often local information—train schedules, show times, restaurant guides—would prove more valuable to consumers than, say, automatic synching with the digital calendars they had been so slow to adopt. At the height of the Internet bubble, these sites weren't the stars of the Internet. But she believed they would be useful to consumers—and, after all, consumers had been her *senmon*, or profession, for her entire career.

Matsunaga's intuition, backed of course by Enoki and DoCoMo's top executives, proved right. Some would argue, in fact, that exposure to the wireless Internet helped catalyze interest in the "real" version. DoCoMo absolutely exploited the luck of developing in an Internetbackward country; but it did so by recognizing the potential, by investing heavily in content plays, and by shifting its focus quickly to the ones that consumers really seemed to want.

2. *DoCoMo was lucky that the banks were in trouble.* Content has driven i-mode's success. And from the very beginning, financial services have been a huge part of that. This may surprise U.S. readers, who have largely ignored electronic bill payment and home banking for well over a decade now. The Japanese have never really embraced the checking culture. Most financial payments were by means of electronic transfers. John remembers signing up for a health club membership in Tokyo in the late 1980s with great trepidation. The club asked for a bank account number so that it could withdraw the money directly every month. To John, this was unheard of—and seemed highly dangerous. The non-paper based nature of bank payments in Japan actually makes Internet banking more appealing there than in the United States.

By the beginning of 2002, there were more than 400 financial institutions delivering services on i-mode, each one providing DoCoMo with not only revenue, but also a compelling reason for consumers to begin using the service. And all that was a stroke of luck, specifically the luck of great timing. Exactly at the moment when i-mode began to seek content partners, the Japanese banking industry was going through its first major consolidation since World War II. "If this had happened ten years ago rather than five years ago," Enoki says, "the banks would not have been interested in talking to us. But as it was, they had all started setting up Internet banking, yet no one was using the service. They were eager to support anything to make this investment work." DoCoMo offered them a new channel.

Of course, the i-mode team had to guess, correctly, that the same consumers who were not using online banking from PCs would for some reason take to it from cell phones. Then the team had to recognize the value this would have to banks. Finally, it had to develop and execute a recruiting strategy to find the right partners—especially, given the conservatism of banks, the right ones to lead the move.

"Sumitomo was the first bank we approached," Enoki explains. "Natsuno led the strategy to get banks on board." Both his ability to communicate with financial types in their own language, and his talent for fleshing out the visions of the new technology, proved invaluable. So did his Internet contacts. According to Enoki, "Natsuno knew many of the people developing systems for the Internet in the financial arena. His theory was that you had to get one of the big name banks on board. Then all the rest would have to follow." Not a shocking assumption—but the right one, and one that Natsuno was able to execute. "Natsuno approached one particular friend and made a proposal. They had a big system for doing banking on the Internet, but no one was using it," Enoki continued.

Two weeks later, a senior vice president from Sumitomo Bank came to visit Enoki and one of DoCoMo's vice presidents. The presence of the DoCoMo VP was critical because, as always in Japan, business had to be conducted at matching organizational levels. Normally, a series of lower-level meetings would have eventually led up to a VP-to-VP meeting. The surprising thing, in this instance, was that his presence was needed so soon.

"I was very touched," Enoki says now. "By sending such a high-level person to talk to DoCoMo, the bank had indicated its strong interest in this project. This meant a lot to us, especially back then. Once Sumitomo had committed, Natsuno could then go to other banks and say 'I can't tell you the name of the bank that has committed to this already, but one of the big banks has and you should, too.'" It worked like a (lucky) charm; when i-mode service launched in January 1999, there were only sixty-seven services listed on the i-mode menu; of these, twenty-one—almost a third!—were financial institutions.

After the launch of i-mode service, it turned out that banking services weren't nearly as popular as some other i-mode content, but the fact that twenty-one of the major financial institutions in Japan supported the launch of i-mode was more than enough to establish a reputation and get it off to a great start. No doubt about it, the lucky break was there, but would it have been there, or would it have produced any change in the world, without the moments of insight and the quick, skillful moves to exploit the opportunity?

3. *DoCoMo was lucky that standards hadn't solidified.* Enoki always brims with pride when he talks about his team. But he has special reason for pride when it comes to technical standards. Standards, of course, are important in many technology markets. They are doubly important when buyers face a lot of rapid change and uncertainty. And they become triply important when the product involves strong network effects (that is, when it's something like a cell phone or fax machine, whose value depends largely on how many other people are part of the same network). So standards are perennially key to mobile commerce. At the same time, they are perennially boring, involving as they do not only technical details but also politics, inside and outside the organization, all in an environment of abstract processes and definitions. Users, content providers, and most managers don't really want to know about standards; if they did, they would have become engineers. Engineers, for their part, understand standards, but they generally have little patience or comfort with the nontechnical discussions they inevitably generate.

So it is no wonder that Enoki is so proud of the young engineer who did a very "un-Japanese" thing during i-mode's development. In a meeting where the WAP standard was being discussed, this junior functionary took on superiors—and from outside his team, to boot. Technical standards hadn't solidified yet, but there was widespread worldwide interest in the WAP format (see Box 4-7). But, in the i-mode team's judgment, the translation of Web pages into WAP readable format was simply too cumbersome. If they were right, this could be a showstopper: A content-driven service where content is perennially outdated or missing is dead in the water.

To avoid this problem, i-mode's technical team had developed what they called compact HTML (cHTML). Other DoCoMo managers and department chiefs had some vested interest in WAP—they had been in early discussions with WAP, and so had technical familiarity, professional pride, and interpersonal face at stake. In this particular meeting, several high-level managers outside the i-mode team were pressuring the i-mode group to accept WAP. But Enoki's young engineer held firm—knowing, of course, that he could count on his boss, who constantly demonstrated noblesse oblige. The engineer explained the team's position respectfully, but without yielding an inch. The payoff? The launching of i-mode with cHTML, which led to richer content, available from more sources, and brought online more quickly. Without the "lucky" culture change that DoCoMo's top executives had created, would this kind of internal conflict have been acceptable? Or would i-mode's prospects have been sacrificed to the corporate need for peaceful coexistence? Fortunately for DoCoMo, we'll never know.

Box 4-7. Is there a WAP in your future?

In Europe, wireless content has been created primarily for WAP-enabled phones. WAP (Wireless Application Protocol) requires that content be converted from HTML (the language that Web pages are written in) to WML (Wireless Mark-up Language). WML is not a natural extension or subset of HTML. But cHTML (the language of i-mode) is so closely related to regular Web site programming that no extra programming is necessary for i-mode devices to read any Web site.

The WAP forum, in which DoCoMo is one of the major players, has promoted a new standard for next generation phones, xHTML. The new standard combines the benefits of XML (the new language of the Internet) and HTML. This standard will allow wireless phones the ability to access Web content easily, using a more rigid structure that cell phones seem to require.

4. *DoCoMo was lucky that Bandai came along.* In the excitement of seeing real sales volume at last, the people watching a new technology often forget that killer apps really don't matter. That is, they don't matter for themselves. The particular value of a killer app is to get users over the hump of trying the new technology, using it enough to see what it's about and—crucially—what else they can do with it. The app itself may not be that important, or valuable, or permanent; once users are comfy with the technology, they may forget about it entirely. That's essentially what happened with VisiCalc (the classic killer app), and indeed with spreadsheets entirely. It's also what happened with screensavers and ringtones.

But while they may not be important for long, when you need those killer apps, you absolutely need them. They are the difference between life and death. And Bandai, the single most important source of killer app content in i-mode's crucial early days, actually stumbled into Enoki's life. "They came to us almost by mistake," he says. "They were not talking about i-mode—people in the outside world didn't know about i-mode yet. Bandai had a machine roughly equivalent to GameBoy. It was called WonderSwan, and Bandai was worried that it wouldn't sell as well as they were hoping. They decided to see if we at DoCoMo could help them put a wireless transmitter on the handset." Bandai was hoping that DoCoMo technology could give them the level of interaction they needed to really drive sales of WonderSwan. Little did they know that the payoff would have nothing to do with their hardware, yet be larger than they imagined.

"Although Bandai came to me," Enoki explains, "this was of course not really my area. I couldn't help them myself, so naturally I referred them to some others internally. But I also took the opportunity to ask them about content that we could include on i-mode." *That* was a well-timed question. It turned out that, in addition to Wonder-Swan, Bandai was already working on a networking game on the conventional Internet. Like Japanese Net use generally, "the game wasn't taking off as fast as they would have liked. But they had the thinking, the servers, and the technical people already in place. They were in an excellent position to get something up and running for i-mode

quickly." In other words, along with commercial interest and atten-
tion-grabbing content, they had pretty much the whole set of attributes that DoCoMo might have dreamed of. "They have become one of
our closest partners on i-mode since."

By now, i-mode's formula seems clear: luck and timing combined
with innovative vision and quick execution. We see the luck, we see
the performance, but we have a hard time distinguishing where one
ends and the other begins. We also note that, after a while, the series of
lucky breaks begins to seem, if not deliberate, then awfully consistent.
Almost as if DoCoMo was somehow manufacturing them...

FIGURE 4-2. Handheld game-console market share in Japan.

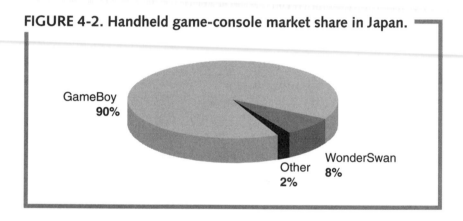

5. *DoCoMo was lucky to have competitors with big egos.* As we
have said, standards discussions bore most of us—but they matter.
For i-mode, they were important not just in opening the market, but
in maintaining, and building on, the much-maligned first mover
advantage. In the beginning, NTT DoCoMo adopted the cHTML
standard. It's principal competitor, J-Phone, adopted MML, which
Enoki believes is a good specification but slightly more difficult to
render than cHTML. In a content-based business with competing
standards, most providers, quite logically, render their content
first for the company with the biggest market share. Then, if it looks

like the content can be profitable, they invest in porting it to multiple platforms.

Because DoCoMo has about 60 percent of the Japanese market, compared to J-Phone's 20 percent, that means DoCoMo consistently has the latest content. And that, of course, helps maintain DoCoMo's lead in market share; all other things being equal, who wants to get the cool new stuff second? That self-perpetuating cycle, though, is not carved in stone, or even in electrons. As Enoki points out, "Mostly, our market share is the limiting factor in this competition. And there is really nothing to stop our competitors from using cHTML except for their egos. So we've been lucky that they haven't decided to adopt it faster than they have."

Enoki prides himself on the lack of ego in NTT DoCoMo. He admits that when DoCoMo releases products to the market, they don't always get the "win." And if a competitor's product is doing better, his company's strategy is simple: "I'll steal it," Enoki says (meaning theft in the artistic sense, of course, not the legal one). For the right kind of person, this humility is a natural outgrowth of time in NTT; the biggest corporation is seldom the most innovative. For many other alumni of market-dominating firms, though, the lesson brought along from the mother ship would have been very different: not the humility to follow, but the arrogance to believe that only solutions "invented here" could be right.

He says that he and his team learn the most from their competitor, J-Phone. "In many instances, we target them. They market directly and strongly to youngsters, teens, and college students. They figure if they can hook them when they are young, they'll have them forever."

"We are constantly learning from J-Phone," Enoki says. "Then we try to incorporate similar offerings into our phone services, along with our existing advantages." The aim is to stay relevant to young people and ultimately to offer greater value, without having to do all the experimentation that a trendsetter has to do.

This requires not just humility and speed, but judgment, as well. For instance, roughly five years ago J-Phone introduced Skywalker service (equivalent to GSM short messaging service). DoCoMo already had a short mail service, but Enoki quickly admitted to himself and his team that it was just not as good. DoCoMo's customers weren't complaining. Most of them felt no need for messaging; they just sent e-mail instead. So taking on the cost and confusion of introducing a true messaging service was not, at that point, the right move. Yet, equally important, Enoki and his team weren't willing to leave well enough alone. Instead, they studied Skywalker and used what they learned to design i-mode e-mail screens to work as simply and effectively as possible, providing more of the value of SMS without literally creating a new system. Staying with their original design just wasn't an option.

"If you don't think like that," Enoki says, you are sunk. "If you aren't willing to change products and services all the time, then you are probably forgetting about customers. If you just lose your ego in the importance you place on customers, then your priorities will always be in the right place."

That sounds simple, almost simplistic. But even in the harshly competitive world of telecomm technology, where advances force rapid convergence toward whatever solution the market prefers, some

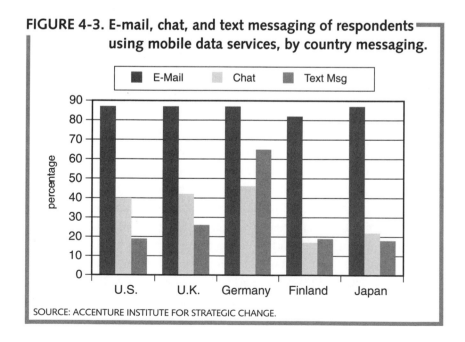

FIGURE 4-3. E-mail, chat, and text messaging of respondents using mobile data services, by country messaging.

SOURCE: ACCENTURE INSTITUTE FOR STRATEGIC CHANGE.

otherwise very successful companies have chosen ego over customers. In about 1997, for example, Enoki remembers being approached by executives at Nokia who complained about the lack of Nokia handset sales in Japan. The executives believed that there had to be some kind of national conspiracy keeping Nokia phones out of the country. Enoki explained that Nokia phones (the smallest in the Western world at the time) were simply too large for the Japanese. He encouraged the executive to make a smaller phone.

Box 4-8. (H)ey you, it's J-Phone.

DoCoMo's two largest competitors in Japan are Au (pronounced "A"-you) and J-phone.

Au (and the smaller Tu-ka) are part of the KDDI group (the former international telecommunications carrier in Japan) which has 23 percent market share in mobile phones.

J-phone (with 17 percent market share) was originally part of Japan Telecom, a postderegulation competitor to NTT. J-phone started as a subsidiary of JR (the Japanese Railroad corporation) and struggled to gain market share, finally gaining prominence through some high-profile deals with AT&T and BT. In 2000, Vodaphone bought 15 percent of the company (from BT) and has steadily upped its share, reaching 67 percent by late 2001. J phone claims the only foreign president of a Japanese telecom, American Daryl Green.

The executive, Enoki remembers, replied that Nokia probably would not make a smaller phone for the Japanese market alone. Westerners were bigger people, they pointed out, with bigger hands;

they therefore needed a bigger phone. Western phones were also much more expensive than the Japanese phones being sold at the time. Fair enough, and that may well have been a very sensible decision based on economies of scale (manufacturing scale, that is, not hand size). On the other hand, phones worldwide seem to have continued shrinking in the years since, Nokia still sells relatively few handsets in Japan, and tech junkies the world over come to Akihabara to see the cutting edge of cell phones. Clearly, these are matters of culture. Isn't it...lucky...that DoCoMo evolved a culture of sacrificing everything, including personal ego, to give customers what they seem to want?

Whistling Past the Telecom Graveyard

How you come down on the whole "lucky versus good" question is, of course, your business. But we believe that the results may be, literally, your business. If you are a leader, a manager, an investor, or even an employee, your judgment here tells you how much to learn, or try to learn, from the DoCoMo team. The same judgment also tells you how to react when good and bad luck comes to your company—and perhaps how to create some luck of your own. But for those involved in telecom, especially wireless, anywhere in the world, it tells you something much more specific: how much to fear DoCoMo's next move.

And here we feel very strongly indeed: *No matter how much luck DoCoMo has had, no matter how foreign i-mode seems to your market, it would be a mistake to discount DoCoMo's success so far, or its prospects in the rest of the world.* If you ignore these guys, you're just not paying attention.

After all, this company has accomplished the most successful consumer technology introduction ever. In three years, starting in a smaller market, it has captured as many Internet users as media behemoth AOL has won in fifteen. Now that it has formed strategic alliances in Europe, North America, and Asia, what's to stop DoCoMo from taking over *your* wireless market?

For many in the telecommunications industry, this is where the question of lucky-or-good becomes deadly serious. Many contend, and many more wish to believe, that DoCoMo's business model and technology are not a threat because i-mode is such a *Japanese* thing. To begin with, they say, the i-mode system was perfectly matched to Japan's culture. It filled a need based largely on commuting patterns found only in the largest cities in the United States and Europe. And the killer apps were things that, try as we might, Westerners are never going to understand. One of the first i-mode celebrities was the perennial Hello Kitty. As an American celebrity might say, "hello!?"

Europeans have fallen in love with SMS

(short messaging service). They exchange an

estimated 10 billion text messages each month.

That averages to about fifty per person every month.

If each message is priced around ten cents,

the "SMS industry" accounts for about

$1 billion in sales in Europe each month.

On top of that, the DoCoMo skeptics contend, i-mode is captive to Japan's technology. DoCoMo only grew so fast in the first place, they say, because there was no mobile phone business yet entrenched in Japan. This allowed the specialized i-mode phones to take hold. But phone users in the United States and Europe have different needs to begin with. And they like the phones they know, the ones made by Western companies like Motorola, Ericsson, and Nokia. These phones really won't run i-mode well. So, the skeptics conclude, since special phones will be necessary for i-mode to run, the conclusion is obvious: i-mode is unlikely to take hold in the rest of the world.

There is certainly something to these basic observations. One look at the most popular wireless content in Japan, the United States, and some European countries (see Figure 4-4) suggests that Japanese culture and society has at least a slight effect on what Japanese Internet users are accessing on their computers and their phones. If the issue is simply choice of content, then the question is: Can a company based in Japan learn to not only meet but even anticipate and sometimes lead the taste of Americans and Europeans in an area they really care about? Even in a market Westerners might regard as a vital part of their culture?

To answer that question, we suggest an exercise: Take a look around the nearest parking lot, especially one used by people who can

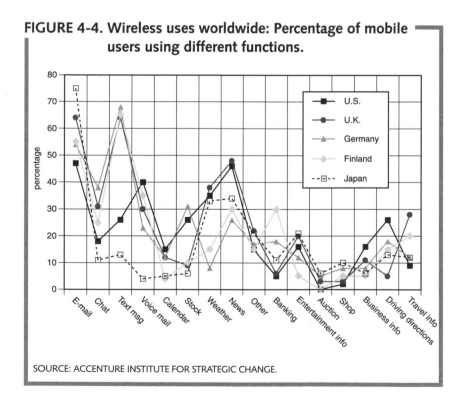

FIGURE 4-4. Wireless uses worldwide: Percentage of mobile users using different functions.

SOURCE: ACCENTURE INSTITUTE FOR STRATEGIC CHANGE.

afford whatever car they want. If the parallel isn't clear, we suggest a drive—perhaps in your RX300, your Miata, or your Acura—to one of the Japanese auto design centers in Southern California, Michigan, or Germay.

OK, so some Japanese firms have proven their ability to lead design in foreign markets. But what if it's not i-mode content, but rather the technology itself that is culture-specific? After all, much of i-mode's success has been attributed to two facts:

- Fact #1: Japanese commute all the time.

- Fact #2: Train riders in Japan are not allowed to talk on cell phones.

So, the argument goes, the Japanese need a mobile text solution to take advantage of all that lost time.

The problem is that neither of these facts is entirely true. There is no doubt that many Japanese in the two largest cities, Osaka and Tokyo, do commute by train. But in the rest of the country, in cities with populations of 500,000 or less, 90 percent of the commuters get back and forth to work by car—just like Americans. And in these less urban areas of Japan, i-mode is selling as well as it is in the cities. What DoCoMo has exploited is not a unique condition of Japanese commuting patterns, but a phenomenon frustratingly familiar to us all: The busier we seem to become, the more "niche time" we seem to face (or at least notice). It's not just commute time, whatever the mode; it's waiting for appointments, standing in line, filling in that half hour until the next class, and so forth.

Likewise, the much-discussed prohibition of talking on mobile phones during train or subway trips is less clear-cut than an i-mode competitor might like. There *are* signs posted that tell people not to turn on their cell phones. But a number of these signs point out that just powering on the phone (whether to talk or handle text messages) poses a risk to people with pacemakers and other medical devices. The real issue is not regulation—we've never heard of anyone being fined for the behavior—so much as etiquette. There are strong *social* sanctions against talking on phones in a crowded train, but no sanctions for quietly tapping away on the keypad. So step onto the platform of a Tokyo train station at rush hour and you'll hear hundreds of mobile phone conversations going on. Step into the railway car, and everyone switches to text.

Things are hardly so uniform in the United States or Europe: When are they ever? But they do seem to be tending in the same direction. We already see increasing social pressure (in theaters, restaurants, schools, even coffeehouses) against extended or loud cell phone conversations. Probably more important, personal and business privacy often makes text messaging more comfortable. And, most important of all, wireless data lets users multitask much more aggressively. Ask any college professor about the side conversations that clearly happen during lectures—without a word being spoken. Japanese commuter etiquette may have helped i-mode take off, but there are much simpler and more universal reasons to adopt some comparable technology just about anywhere.

The story for killer apps is much the same. Yes, the screensavers and ringtones that drove initial i-mode action in Japan are fairly culture-specific. It's hard for us to imagine American executives using Bandai gorilla screen savers or *anything* related to Hello Kitty. But then again, the population that takes wireless data into the mainstream in Europe or North America may not be executives at all. It may be young people, just as it was in Japan. And characters like Hello Kitty, Pokemon, and the Asterix gang—to say nothing of all those Disney and Hanna Barbera standbys—are sold everywhere in the world.

Equally important, serious Western business types can develop little data addictions of their own, sometimes to the oddest streams of fast-changing and arguably trivial data. Remember Pointcast? Ever watch Sports Center? When was the last time you drove a car without a radio? And don't get us started on games: interactive Tetris, anyone? As for ringtones and screensavers more generally, it's true; so far, Americans aren't buying. But Europeans, and non-Japanese East Asians, absolutely are.

Having looked at wireless data use on three continents we are absolutely convinced that culture matters. But we are equally convinced that the critical issue is finding the *right* application, not assuming there won't be one. We're not sure that DoCoMo will be first to find the killer app for mobile commerce in the United States or Europe, but given their record in Japan, we wouldn't bet against them.

If culture won't keep DoCoMo out, what about technology? That might be a barrier. The argument is that the technology Japan uses for i-mode (PDC) won't work well on phones used in the rest of the world (which mainly depend on GSM and CDMA). And knowing how demanding consumers are, and how unhappy they are even with the relatively universal technologies behind wireless voice, we can easily imagine the wrong technology scuttling an effort at Western expansion.

But will DoCoMo use the wrong technology? Or is this simply an assumption flowing from the history (and pride) of Western phone manufacturers? In the past, unlike the kind of car company that might send left-hand-drive cars to a right-hand-drive country, DoCoMo has been energetic in using the technology that seemed most appropriate. Some of i-mode's design *did* emerge from the small size of Japanese cell phones. In 1997, Chris Patridge of London's *The Evening Standard* described these phones as "tiny, almost jewel-like" and marveled at their price tag of between ten and fifty British pounds.[3] So there was already a tradition of very sleek, slim phones in Japan on which i-mode was forced to build. They made technical and design choices to accommodate that hardware. But we've seen that in doing so, they were very resourceful and creative.

In entering global markets, DoCoMo has at least two promising choices. First, they could be equally resourceful in adapting their system to the local hardware of choice. Second, they could offer Japan's current handset technology, evolved now to be even tinier and possibly even more jewel-like, to users in the West. After all, changing hardware may not be the barrier one might assume. Customers in the United States already think of the cellular handset and service as a matched pair. Certainly, neither of us wants to count the number of cell phones we have been through. Think we're exceptions? Look at

Box 4-9. How leading analysts think of mobile data.

"U-commerce has the power to reshape whole industries and create a future that is altogether different from today's m-commerce, mobile commerce, world."

"U-commerce has several defining characteristics:

- It is a world where economic activity is *u*biquitous, *un*bounded by the traditional definitions of commerce, and *u*niversal with everyday, around-the-clock broadband connectivity.
- It is a world where every platform—the Internet, mobile devices, embedded sensors—interfaces with everything else.
- It is a world where mobile devices—*u*niting features of the wireless phone, Palm organizer, PC, and two-way pager—become the one thing individuals cannot live without."

"In the always-on world of u-commerce, the real value of the *e* and *m* will be realized. U-commerce is not a replacement for anything companies are doing today, but an extension of it. And it will be mandatory, not optional."

"U-commerce is about major change, and the risks will hit everyone, sooner or later. The rewards will go to those who move aggressively, and effectively, to embrace the changes."

"Prospective players can expect stunning growth. The global market for wireless Internet-capable devices is set to grow 630 percent by 2005, by which time there will be more than 1.7 billion mobile connections. In the United States alone, m-commerce

> transactions will be a $20 billion business. For those able to leverage the unique quality of these devices and tailor services and products that tap into the customer's location, context, and personal preferences, the opportunities are staggering."
>
> SOURCE: ACCENTURE

the people around you. If they use a cell phone at all, how old does the handset look? Is it their first? How much would it cost them to replace it, if they switched carriers or renewed a contract at the same time? And think about a technology less likely to be subsidized, the PDA: Of your colleagues who use one at all, how many are still using their first?

Finally, think about the demographics of technology users. In the United States, college students and those just starting out in their careers are much more likely than the rest of us to have cell phones and other not-quite-standard technology. What if, outside its home market, DoCoMo borrowed not J-Phone's features but its strategy, concentrating on young people buying their first grown-up mobile device? That might leave them without the supposedly lucrative business market, at least for a while. But even if DoCoMo "only" won a generation of enthusiastic and sophisticated technology users, customers with fifty years of data to send and retrieve...what would be the consolation prize? So, given their history and even the small set of options we outsiders can see, what do you think? Is DoCoMo likely to falter over culture and technology?

Getting Lucky: A Beginner's Guide

After a whole chapter on DoCoMo's lucky breaks, we hope you'll allow us a small, and perhaps instructive, personal confession: The reason we first saw DoCoMo making its own luck is that we've seen it in our own projects and organizations. We've both worked long enough at different organizations to learn that there are lucky and unlucky firms. Sometimes the luck seems completely external; other times it's easy to see how the attitudes and attentiveness of the people inside create or exploit lucky breaks. But the clearest lesson is that there are patterns, and they really matter.

We even see that in ourselves. We have the good fortune of being very different people when it comes to luck. Over a twenty-year friendship, we've come to see (and our common friends delight in pointing out) that John makes enough luck for several people. He naturally expects good things to happen, watches for them, and moves quickly to exploit them when they do. Mitch, on the other hand, seems to manufacture the other kind. Not where it really counts; on the big stuff, like family, health, friends, and work, Mitch is a bona fide lucky guy. But on little things, this guy radiates misfortune.

The definitive experiment, conducted years ago, was sending him out to hitch a ride from one end of Martha's Vineyard to the other. Remember, this was before the term "serial killer" had even been invented; it was off the coast of Cape Cod, where hitchhiking was a time-honored tradition; it was near a town where he'd been working for months; and it was on a genteel and friendly little island in the middle of summer. In other words, the experimental conditions were as laid-back a setting as New England has to offer. To further stack the odds in Mitch's favor, the experiment even included an attractive and cheerful female traveling companion—always good for roadside attention and reassurance that the guy must be OK—and just enough rain to make anyone with a soul take pity on the poor (but clean cut!) wayfaring strangers. Anyone else would have been picked up in a minute. John, traveling by himself with a five-day stubble, would have been picked up by his future soulmate, who would just happen to be rich, beautiful, charming, and deeply interested in Asian business. Mitch stood there for hours, somehow creating an invisible force field that rendered the young couple invisible to passing motorists. They finally walked the entire length of the island, though we should point out (there's his luck in big things again) that the girl is still with him. She's learned, though, that Mitch is not the guy to buy a lottery ticket with. (*From*, maybe, but not with.) The most important fact, though, is that this outcome surprises no one who knows them. It fits Mitch's luck profile perfectly.

We bet you've got similar experiences yourself. Once you have enough information, it just becomes clear that luck matters, and some people have more than their share of it.

How can you make your organization one of these lucky ones? There are no guarantees, of course; after all, luck is *supposed to be* mysterious. But DoCoMo's experience, seen from the inside, suggests that you build on five principles:

1. *Luck is not just a random event.* By now it's obvious that we really believe in, as Davies puts it, "making things happen to us." (What can we say, it's all those years in Southern California and the mystic Southwest.) But you don't have to sign on for that. You can reject "making luck" entirely. Just remember that for every one of DoCoMo's lucky breaks, the value came not just because the luck occurred, but because someone in the company recognized it and jumped—quickly and with vision—to turn that event to the firm's advantage. If that's the behavior you need, then what you want to build is an organization that, like John, *expects good things to happen, watches for them, and moves quickly to exploit them when they do.*

2. *But you do need lucky external events.* Even if you believe that people make good things happen to them, you have to remember—we certainly do—that they can't usually pick and choose those things in advance. The lucky moments that helped i-mode break out of the wireless data pack are not mainly ones that anyone would have anticipated, chosen, or even thought about. Who knew that Bandai or the banks would need i-mode just when it came along? Or even that Japanese buyers would see wireless Net access with a tiny screen and keyboard as more desirable (even with its cost advantage) than what Yasuko calls "the real Internet"? No one. So being lucky doesn't mean picking battles and insisting that you'll win each one; it includes reflexive optimism, but also cutting your losses and ignoring potential lucky breaks (like enthusiasm from i-modes's early business users) that just didn't pan out.

3. *You can't fight culture.* A clear lesson from DoCoMo's experience is that the culture of any group influences its behavior. This influence seems especially powerful in those hazy areas like recognizing a lucky break when you see it, or innovating, or knowing when to push (like pitching i-mode to Bandai, when what they asked for was a gaming platform). So you need to understand what your group's culture is and what it would need to be, to make the kind of luck (or deliver any kind of performance) that you want. If there's a gap, you need to think seriously about whether this group can vault over it. Perhaps, instead, you should spin off a group that can invent the kind of culture needed (that seems to have worked pretty well for NTT, which still owns 64 percent of the biggest success story from Asia in a decade). Or, if you need to change culture internally, recognize the kind of investment that will be required, not in workshops and mission statements, but in bringing in the kind of people, like Enoki and Matsunaga, whom the culture can crystallize around—and protecting them from the existing culture's defenses.

4. *No matter how lucky you are, you still need leadership.* DoCoMo was lucky in finding people like Enoki; in inheriting useful technologies; in facing opponents who are easy to copy from and not enthusiastic at copying from others, even when it would help. But each lucky break had to be exploited. Equally important, that culture had to be developed. And all that flowed from the very top, via noblesse oblige. Giving your people the confidence, the resources, and the freedom to make their own luck requires delivering what the military guys call "top cover." No one can manufacture luck in the marketplace while defending themselves from constant, internal attacks— especially if those come from the boss.

5. *Luck comes from people.* We wouldn't advocate lotteries or massive coin-toss contests in hiring; if we did, people like Mitch would never find a job. And the kind of luck-making you need in business is too complex and situational to really test. But that means you have to be obsessive about making the right matches. Think carefully about the kind of person who could "make luck" in the jobs you need to fill: Enoki was lucky at hiring creative people, Matsunaga at instilling a creative culture, and so forth. Invest whatever you have to in finding, recruiting, and protecting those people. Show them by example that yours is a lucky organization. And support them, not only in making their own group's luck, but in transmitting that attitude throughout the ranks. Remember the junior engineer who stood up against WAP? That was a very lucky day for DoCoMo. There wasn't time for him to check with the boss before facing down his higher-ranking internal opponents. So he had to have confidence, going in, that his group would generally have good luck—in technology, in corporate politics, and in the marketplace. By believing in that, he helped make it true. *That's* leading through passion.

Notes

1. Christopher Jencks et al., *Inequality: A Reassessment of the Effect of Family and Schooling in America* (New York: Basic Books, 1972).
2. Nancy Koehn, *Brand New: How Entrepreneurs Earned Consumers' Trust from Wedgwood to Dell* (Boston, Ma.: Harvard Business School Press, 2001).
3. Chris Patridge, "Gizmo Heaven in Tokyo," *The Evening Standard*, November 10, 1997.

CHAPTER FIVE

Fun

"Work is much more fun than fun."
—NOËL COWARD

TIME FOR SOME BRUTAL HONESTY HERE. Time, too, for some not-quite-PC remarks. As people outside business seem to have just discovered, we live in a shrinking world. You're reading a whole book about DoCoMo, which is as big as Internet success stories get...but it is still a Japanese company. You wouldn't be here unless you were a cosmopolitan, global kind of thinker. So we know you're not the kind of person to stoop to cultural stereotypes. Neither are we.

Still, this book is written purely for a Western audience. (The Japanese don't have to read about DoCoMo; they're surrounded by it.) So, just between us *gaijin* (foreigners), when you saw the title of this chapter, wasn't your first response, "Yeah, right. *Fun* in a business book—a Japanese business book? In what galaxy?"

That reaction may not be diplomatic...but it's very common. And with good reason. We don't know any culture where managers and executives talk much about the importance of fun in their business. Whether you're briefing Wall Street analysts, recruiting great employees, or rallying the troops, other motivations just seem more...businesslike. So executives talk about "maximizing shareholder value" and

147

"dominating our sector." In less aggressive climates, maybe the emphasis is on quality or even tradition. But fun is not a big part of the mission statement.

If you probe most business types, they'll admit to having fun. In fact, they can even be a little defensive about it. But the fun they're talking about is far outside the office. It's used as a badge of shared humanity; sharing a few hours at a sporting event is great for team-building...so we'll be more productive. Or it's on the other side of the great equation—the one that the invention of money made possible. We all work hard to create value, which we can translate into money, which we can then translate into (that's the whole point of currency) *almost anything we want.* When you get over to that other side ("the demand side"), there's plenty of business conversation about fun. In flush times, there are the fancy cars and boats; the trips; the summer places. There are the luxury goods written up in *Forbes* and *Smart Money:* cigars, SUVs, motorcycles. In business, that's the stuff that is supposed to be fun.

Back in the New Economy boom, there was another kind of fun, too—fun at work. Remember? Offices that looked like the set of *Friends,* in-house pool tables, magically restocked refrigerators. But even then, would you really tell a senior exec, an investor, or even an employee that "the main reason to do this is that it's gonna be fun"?

When you move that question to Japan, things get even more serious—at least to our Western eyes. Some of that difference is pure propaganda, left over from the days of Japan, Inc. (see Box 5-1). Millions of Americans, though they've never been to Japan and never worked with any Japanese nationals, have a very strong image of Japanese business: powerful brands built through patient capital, government-industry collaboration, and, most important, an unending supply of tireless workers who will do anything for the cause—the kamikazes of the corporate world. Work twenty hours a day? They'll do it. Give up weekends and holidays? No problem! Take pay cuts every time their customers run into economic trouble and can't pay as much? Absolutely! Spend practically nothing, so that banks have plenty of capital to lend to corporations? Of course! Superhuman, perhaps, but definitely *not* fun.

> ## Box 5-1. Japan, Inc.
>
> From the West's point of view, the Japanese boom of the 1980s was built on the auto industry. The decade opened with Chrysler and Ford literally fighting for survival as a slew of Japanese imports—cheaper, better, and much more fuel efficient—won a huge share of the U.S. market. The endangered members of the Big Three survived, but the decade still ended with America's political leaders begging the Japanese to buy more of our left-side-drive automobiles. A whole generation came to grips with the idea that Japan—the country it had defeated in World War II—was ready to take over the economic world. Another generation accepted Sony and Honda as symbols of innovation, style, and quality, as obvious in their leadership as Cadillac had been to their parents.

Naturally, there was a rhetorical response. Lest Americans and Europeans panic about the Japanese miracle—which genuinely was a miracle—an entire industry grew up teaching Westerners about Japan's deficiencies. First and foremost, we were told, they didn't play fair. American industry was in favor of free global trade, but only with the famous "level playing field." Nearly as important was the contention, which had its roots decades earlier, that the Japanese could manufacture really well, but they just couldn't innovate. Despite products like the Walkman, despite industries like numeric-controlled machine tools and robotics, despite design and process changes that completely reset quality and efficiency standards, the Japanese were supposed to be basically just copycats. Finally, there was the stereotype of the people: kamikaze producers at home, inexplicable and rather nerdy (if deep-pocketed) tourists abroad. They just weren't a fun gang.

There may even be truth to some of these claims. But just for the record, reality was quite a bit different. Since life is too short to spend much time on the trade battles of a bygone era, simply ask yourself two questions. First, if you had to choose between the typical American car of the 1980s or its Japanese equivalent—which would you buy? Second, of all the high-tech devices you've bought, how many come from Japan, and why?

The question of fun is a bit more subtle. That's no problem for John; having grown up in Utah, he's an expert at finding nonglamorous fun. And he's here to report that the Japanese are, in fact, every bit as fun-loving as Americans. They just compartmentalize—like Westerners do, but to a far greater extreme. The business veneer is no nonsense, but still waters run deep.

This is, after all, the place that invented karaoke. It's the home of the *Iron Chef,* not to mention game shows far weirder than *Survivor, Temptation Island,* and *The Chair* all rolled into one. Drinking with colleagues, the most common way of breaking through that veneer, is almost mandatory. Entertainment budgets would make an American CPA blush. And it shouldn't be any surprise to Americans who have visited Japan why this island nation dominates the animation and video game markets—on any subway train you'll find a surprising number of middle-aged business people (mostly men) reading comic books; ditto their number in video arcades.

To be fair, the no-fun stereotype isn't entirely made up. If you've ever met a group of Japanese businesspeople on a foreign fact-finding mission, you know the routine. They focus in on a limited number of facts or suppositions and ask question after question about a single point. They won't challenge you; they won't refute you; they won't ask about the "big picture"; they're after details. In their own factories and offices, most Japanese businesspeople display similar tendencies. Lots of detail, lots of small improvements, lots of dedication...not a whole lot of visible fun.

Yet when you look closely at DoCoMo's story, fun is absolutely central. As with other Japanese phenomena, it's not always out there on the surface. But it's a huge part of what sets the company apart from competitors, not just in the home market but all over the globe. Without fun, i-mode could never have bucked the odds to create such a huge market while the rest of the Japanese economy was setting new records for stagnation. Likewise, whatever you think of the "Japan can't innovate" stereotype generally, it's clear that someone forgot to tell DoCoMo. Since its inception, it has been one of the most successfully innovative firms in the entire high-tech world. Innovation always depends on a lot of factors, but we're convinced that fun has been vital for DoCoMo's innovation—and could be equally fruitful for many other firms, no matter where they are located.

One of These Things Is Not Like the Other

We can hear you already. "Fun is nice," you're saying, "No problem there. But there's a reason they call it work. It's a tough market out there, and fun isn't what the market wants. Maybe it worked for one strange Japanese company, but that sure doesn't mean it's right for MY team."

You may be right. But, as you'll see, DoCoMo's experience is not all that unusual; it's much closer to normal than are the company's stratospheric results. Their challenges, and their responses, are probably more like yours—or more like yours ought to be—than you think.

But don't take our word for it. Don't even take DoCoMo's example. When it comes to the business value of fun, the best way to understand the i-mode experience is to look closely at your own. Think carefully about four specific moments of truth in your own career; then decide whether fun might be just the feeling you need to manage for.

Moment of Truth #1
Your First Real Job

As a teenager, you probably fantasized about an outrageous career: professional athlete, rock star, maybe even business tycoon. Don't worry if that seems unrealistic now; you were, after all, young. But there's more to those youthful dreams than most people admit. Sure, part of the appeal was flat-out glamour: As Mark Knopfler put it in the song, "money for nothing, chicks for free." But even then, weren't you drawn to something deeper, too? Wasn't part of your passion related to the work itself—freedom, power, artistry, self-expression? And in those days, when you took your dreams seriously, you were different. At least a part of you was driven, committed, even obsessed. In your mind, and in at least some of your actions, you devoted enormous, concentrated effort to a single pursuit. Add it up: how many hours did you practice basketball? How many bruises did you collect learning skateboarding? How much esoteric information did you memorize about the music or sport or whatever it was that had captured your heart? You were creative then, too—full of ideas.

All that passion, commitment, and potential was there, in your heart and head, just waiting to be focused on your calling. Maybe it wouldn't have been rock music or professional sports. But you were ready, willing, and able to be—to make yourself—a star in your career.

Then came your first real job.

Whether it was flipping burgers in high school or cranking out spreadsheets after college, it was a long way from your dream. Sure, you were excited to get that job, whether for the money, the social value, or the challenge. But unless you were very, very lucky, the excitement quickly turned into a grind.

From work that made you amazingly happy, the focus abruptly shifted to keeping someone else happy: your boss, your customers, maybe your creditors with that paycheck. And before long, the transaction had become second nature: you got money, but what you traded was unhappiness by the hour. Your fun was mostly unrelated (goofing off) or even subversive (bonding with coworkers...but *against* the company, boss, or customers). Fun—excitement, creativity, the pleasure of hitting it hard just because you could—all that went out the window. And with it went a ton of value that you could have created for your firm and its customers downstream.

Can You Be Creative and Work at the Same Time?
The good news is that, as you moved up in your career, things got more fun and (not coincidentally) more productive. The bad news is

that your experience wasn't unique then, isn't unique now...and is not confined to anyone's first job. In the summer of 2000, we surveyed 1,000 employees of a major multinational firm. The firm is respected, does high-quality work, and consistently achieves good results in the marketplace. But for reasons that will become obvious, it wishes to remain anonymous.

We asked these workers, who were mainly professionals or staff with significant technical skills, how much support they could expect from their company, their bosses, and their coworkers. If they had a great idea, could they count on interest and buy-in? Very few expected high levels of support.

We also asked them to rank creativity:

- Their own innate abilities, measured when they were children

- Their ability to create now, as adults, after years of socialization through school and work

- The creative ability of their peers

- The creativity of the organization as a whole

As Figure 5-1 on the following page illustrates, the results formed a depressing, unsurprising, and slippery slope. These professionals saw themselves as fairly creative by nature. But they were constrained in using that creativity in adult life; they were dragged down by less creative peers; and most importantly they were boxed in by an organization that is sharply less creative than the people who make it up.

Of course, that's based on self-assessments. If you assume that these professionals are fairly accurate in their judgments, then it's clear that a huge amount of potential—the energy to create new value—is lost, hidden, or repressed by our organizations. Having spent some time in all kinds of organizations, private and public, large and small, we suspect this is true. But even if we choose not to believe the self-assessments, one thing is undeniable: Professional employees *believe* that even an enlightened, thriving, well-managed organization can't take advantage of their full potential...or maybe doesn't even want to.

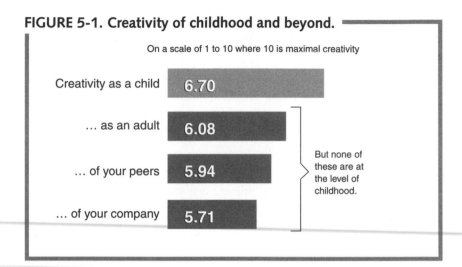

FIGURE 5-1. Creativity of childhood and beyond.

On a scale of 1 to 10 where 10 is maximal creativity

Creativity as a child — 6.70

... as an adult — 6.08

... of your peers — 5.94

... of your company — 5.71

But none of these are at the level of childhood.

As a manager, as a senior executive, as an investor: Is there any doubt in your mind that employees who feel that way about their jobs are "leaving money on the table"—money in the form of creativity, productivity, commitment, product quality? Is there any doubt about their loyalty? About their performance when you need them most?

Mari-bucho Tries to Have Fun

DoCoMo—a company whose performance goes beyond extraordinary—strives for a very different outcome. There is an implicit belief that employees who find fun in their work, who actually take joy from doing their jobs, are great employees.

At DoCoMo, fun flowed from the i-mode leadership team, which was hired mostly from outside DoCoMo. From Day One, Mari Matsunaga, who led the team, had a very different sense of priorities and proprieties from those who had been raised in NTT. It didn't hurt that Enoki (who had once aspired to being a "sit-down" comedian, see Box 5-2) led the team. But wit and personality alone didn't do the job; Matsunaga also brought to the nascent team a unique set of business practices.

> ## Box 5-2. Japanese sit-down comedy.
>
> *Rakugo* is a form of Japanese comic storytelling with hundreds of years of history. The stories consist of dialogues, with a single performer playing several characters. Generally, *Rakugo* themes concern themselves with traditional Japanese culture and society in the eighteenth century. Think of those dusty folktales from grade school but told by a kneeling Chris Rock clad in traditional Japanese attire.

Mari set the tone by insisting that everyone call her by her first name. This was such a leap, in the Japanese setting, that some of her subordinates just couldn't make it. They omitted the family name, all right, but made up for it by appending the honorific "department chief," and so she became Mari-bucho. The fun really started when Mari suggested an off-site "brainstorming" session at the Hotel Seiyo. Her new DoCoMo staff members—the people who would invent the first mobile data service that somehow attracted a mass consumer audience—had never even heard the term brainstorming. Once they got past the innovativeness of this concept, they experienced even greater culture shock with the entertainment and publishing industry cronies that Matsunaga invited.

Nothing as Fun as Having a Concierge

Matsunaga remembers in her book *The Birth of i-mode* that at one point in the brainstorming, her "industry" friends started talking about how nice it was to get away to a hotel to lounge around during the middle of the working day. She said that by this kind of "joking, then returning to serious discussion, I could feel my brain coming alive." In the course of the banter, the group talked about their favorite hotel services, and one of the participants mentioned that she liked the "concierge" service the most. This comment stuck in Matsunaga's mind. She decided right then and there that what i-mode really needed to be was a digital concierge—helping you to perform all the bothersome tasks of life when you are away from home. Of course, it turned out that this concierge concept, not the supercharged Palm Pilot or the businessperson's tool, would drive the use of wireless data in Japan.

No one could have predicted that a side conversation—the least productive part of a radically unproductive-looking day—would hold the key to DoCoMo's future. Yet Mari knew—as we do, as you do, if you'll reflect on your own experience—that the human mind operates under a kind of reverse Murphy's Law; the answers you really need come from the places you least expect. That observation is common; what is rare is the courage to take the next step. Mari, and soon DoCoMo, took the plunge. If answers come from outside "work," then the people you are trusting to produce answers need to spend more time playing.

Matsunaga made a point of the benefits of this kind of informal "play session." And her bosses took note. Soon after the Hotel Seiyo brainstorming session, Enoki rented an additional room for brainstorming in the building where the i-mode team was housed. When Enoki first ushered her into the room, Matsunaga was surprised to find it furnished with comfortable couches and mahogany furniture. A refrigerator in one of the cabinets was well stocked with alcohol. There was even a karaoke machine.

The room, which Enoki dubbed Club Mari, was an immediate and lasting success. Club Mari somehow enabled people to tap into the same kind of passion and creativity we all found in our youthful dreams—and yet to focus that energy on the challenges their business faced today. Over the coming months, as i-mode took shape, some of the most important business decisions in the history of NTT DoCoMo were made in this less-than-businesslike room. The total cost (the room, the ambience, even the time that DoCoMo staffers spent there) might have been, what, a hundred thousand dollars? Or even half a million, screaming maximum? The ideas worked out there helped DoCoMo create billions for its investors.

Moment of Truth #2
The Last Time You Gave 100 Percent at Work

DoCoMo invested in fun; the return was tremendous performance. But it's important to understand that those results did not flow just from a loyal workforce that spent some work time relaxing. Much more was involved...and woven through the center, once more, was fun.

Fun, it turns out, makes you smarter. Not simply more creative, but just plain better at all the decisions and actions it takes to make any business fly. Why should that be? To see how fun boosts performance—what it did for DoCoMo's daily operation, and what it can do for just about anyone's—go back to your own experience, to another moment of truth. *Think about the last time that work, of any kind, actually felt like play.* What was that like? Allow us, fresh from interviews at DoCoMo, to speculate:

- You were giving 100 percent effort but didn't feel strain.

- You were taking smart risks.

- You were creative.

- You blew past people, on your own team or the competition, who weren't also "in the zone."

In short, your performance was great, in personal-best territory, because you were fully engaged.

Let's be clear: This is *not* just a case of "the team that wants it more." For the level of performance you experienced, there has to be some element of genuine playfulness, some transcendence of carrots and sticks and worrying about the outcome. The focus has to shift to intrinsic experience of the work itself; in short, the work becomes fun.

It Feels Like a Job
It's a common point that geniuses, artists, and inventors think of their work as play—sometimes painful, sometimes obsessive, but play.

What we can tell you, after years in think tanks and universities and high-powered consulting firms, is that the same holds true for hundreds of people who are perhaps less celebrated but still very, very smart. For the high performers in those environments, that kind of attitude is so common that it might almost be a requirement. And it's not just intellectuals who work this way.

When American football star Joe Montana retired from his sport at age thirty-eight, he told the 20,000 people who turned out for his street party the reason he quit: because "it felt like a job." In other words, when he was making those incredible plays that inspired fans all over the country, plays they remember even today, it didn't feel like work. It felt like play. From yet a different perspective, Dr. Thomas Stanley, who has run multivariate regressions on the factors that help predict who will establish high net worth, says that this approach to work is near the top of the list. "Millionaires love their careers," he wrote. "As one of our wealthier members stated, 'It is not work; it is a labor of love.'"[1]

...or Not

Naturally, what feels like play is different for each person. Mitch and John both know otherwise normal people who actually have fun making columns of numbers add up. Intellectually, we see the appeal: the symmetry, the precision, the feeling of order and control. Emotionally, though, you couldn't pay us enough to do that. So the probability that we would ever feel that this work is play—no matter how hard we try, or how well it's going—is minuscule. Al Hirschfeld, one of the most famous cartoonists of the twentieth century, put it this way. "People just enjoy different things. I'm not a great nature lover, and I'm terrible at sight-seeing. But when I'd come back from Paris, I would sit for hours in the window of Howard Johnson's at the corner of Broadway and Forty-sixth Street making little sketches, watching people go by. I find that stimulating." For him, sketching in HoJo's was fun. And that's the key.

Of course, some (unenlightened and not particularly generous) people will argue that fun is great for stars, and artists, and geniuses—

but not for the rest of the team. We suspect that these people have not taken a close look recently at the kind of performance required, at every level, to make any commercial organization function. The bar has gone way, way up. For high performance, you need a whole team of people to make a bunch of pretty impressive, not quite logical (but really *valuable*) leaps, judgments, and decisions. Your geniuses can invent and strategize all they want, but the people on the ground have to be innovative, flexible, and smart in implementing the grand plan. Otherwise, failure is pretty much assured.

That's one of the most positive and valuable lessons from the dot-com boom (and bust): the thrill and great performance you can get from a startup. When you're part of a brand new enterprise, whether it's a new company or the team behind a new product, the underlying challenge is that EVERYTHING is being invented from scratch. So you've got people at every level of the team making snap decisions about how this will work. You don't have the time or resources to study and vet each decision; you have to hope that their instincts will be good. There are invisible, daily decisions, way below the level of corporate strategy, that ultimately add up to some of the biggest bets the enterprise will ever make. For an effort like i-mode, there was the dance of knowing which features to offer and how to fine tune them (like deciding to streamline e-mail, rather than building in stand-alone SMS capabilities); there was the eternal question of when one aspect of quality had reached "good enough," allowing effort to shift to some other aspect; there were all kinds of marketing and pricing and engineering decisions that depended on instinctive guesses about what trade-offs customers would make when comparing i-mode to the competition.

All these challenges, and many more, were faced not only by DoCoMo's top execs and the i-mode team leadership, but by ordinary employees. One at a time, bit by bit, sometimes without realizing it, they created and limited DoCoMo's options. The same kinds of decisions are made by ordinary employees all over the world every day. It's not just in new markets, and not just in high tech. The clerk on the sales floor, the service tech out in the field, the worker on the line—

they all have to decide, minute by minute, how to adapt, because the challenges your company faces change in small but important ways all the time.

And just like i-mode's employees, those ordinary workers face risk, as well. There's the risk of being wrong. There is the risk that the enterprise—the project, the team, or the company—will literally fail. (When the popular press reports that the average millionaire entrepreneur goes bankrupt 3.75 times, and when one of the most visible and politically connected firms in the country evaporates seemingly overnight, taking with it an accounting firm that was literally part of the business landscape, then people realize that failure is always an option—and not just a theoretical one.) There is the risk that comes with knowing, as everyone has learned by now, that the company cannot offer them security, even when their daughter is about to get married, or their parents need an assisted-living center, or it's time for the big anniversary trip to Paris. There are a hundred things, or a thousand, that they could possibly be worrying about. For sustained high performance, you need the people on your team not to worry about any of that. You need them operating in the zone we talked about earlier—what Mihaly Csikszentmihalyi calls "a flow state."[2] You need them fully engaged.

Fun Gets Them There

Why is fun so important?

■ *First, because fun is a powerful antidote to risk.* High performance work is inherently risky. If you're fully engaged, you are by definition taking things to their limits. You're competing. You're trying new stuff. Fun is a natural way of outweighing those risks and, more important, helping you forget they even exist. Fun promotes the attitude that Michael Schrage calls "ready/fire/aim," an attitude he links to companies with high levels of innovation.[3]

■ *Second, fun encourages adaptive behavior.* If you're engaged, you are constantly monitoring, almost with your subconscious, the things going on around you. You're adjusting. You're evolving. You're dealing with the problem of the moment, quickly and flexibly. What could be a better prescription for high performance? And, as Robert Fagen says, having fun is a great way of preparing for the kind of engagement, as well as practicing it. "In a world continuously presenting unique challenges and ambiguity, play prepares [us] for an evolving planet."

■ *Third, fun helps silence the internal critics.* In *Finding Your Own North Star*, best-selling author Martha Beck points out that we perform best when we are being true to our essential selves—the "you" that is deep inside.[4] That's harder than it sounds, she explains, because we have spent years (for some pretty good reasons), constructing what she calls our "social self"—the part of us that is an expert in what it takes to get approval, and why that matters. Many of us do such a good job that it takes real effort to get back to our essential selves—even when the obedient social self says that that's the right thing to do. Fundamentally, *Finding Your Own North Star* suggests bribing the social self to stop being such a spoilsport and let the essential self work (which happens whenever we are fully engaged). Fun is the best bribe, and distraction, we can think of.

■ *Fourth, fun provides perspective.* People who are very serious about high performance, like Phil Jackson, who coached both Michael Jordan and the league-dominating L.A. Lakers, look to Zen and similar philosophies to help them reach their highest professional potential. One of the concepts they talk about most is getting distance from the activity—forgetting the self, observing the activity, and being fully in the moment. That's obviously the kind of full engagement we're talking about. And while we believe that meditation, or yoga, would be a great way of getting there, we know for sure that fun does it. When you're having fun, you're not worrying about the outcome or yourself.

■ *Fifth, fun lets you "putt like a kid."* Trust us, you don't need to be a golfer to appreciate this one. Mitch, nearly as good a golfer now as Tiger Woods was at age 4, loves James Dobson's advice that every would-be golfer should "putt like a kid." If you do, you will not miss your putts because you hit them timidly. You won't irritate your companions and yourself by overanalyzing every shot. And you won't suffer from what golfers call the yips—a nervous condition, truly dreaded by professionals and weekend players alike. When you have the yips, you care so much about the outcome, and the fear of failure is so strong in your mind, that you more or less create the failure you're worried about.

That doesn't happen to kids. It's not because they want to win more, or less, than adults do. It's because they are *playing* golf, not working at it. Left to their own devices, kids don't see anything to be afraid *of* in knocking a little white ball ten or twenty feet into a hole. Their heads aren't full of instructions, and limits, and complexities. They seem unable to even imagine a complicated chain of hopes and fears that somehow connects that little tiny ball to their worth as human beings. So they play from the heart. They don't always make their putts, but they always *play* them. That's what fun will do for you.

Recapturing the FUN of Childhood

Even a newly-hooked (as opposed to newly-sliced) golfer like Mitch can see the business value here. Kids are unparalleled in the force of their enthusiasm, in their ability to engage fully (even if only for a very short period), and in remembering that most things are really no big deal. We can't think of many adults who wouldn't be better at their jobs if they could somehow recapture that.

For those who find all this uncomfortably reminiscent of "inner child" discussions, two notes. First, neither of us is presently wearing a crystal, magnet, or talisman of any kind. We don't even really know what chakras are. Second, you can learn the same lesson from a source so respectable that every U.S. president has to have one: a dog. Who knows where the phrase "work like a dog" came from? Sure, dogs perform wonderfully important and complicated jobs—tracking lost hikers, helping the police avoid deadly force, guiding the disabled, herding uncooperative sheep. But when was the last time you saw a dog that wasn't having fun, even if he was working? That's their secret; they have pretty much the same expression, pretty much the

> ## Box 5-3. What is it about golf anyway?
>
> Anyone who happens not to golf—hint, hint—and who hangs around business for long could easily grow tired of, or at least be mystified by, all the talk about this particular game. What's the deal? Well, as your humble golf-challenged authors have pieced it together, it turns out that golf really is a good analogy to business. It's a game that many people actually participate in, as adults. It combines technique, strategy, execution, and the need to bear up under random events that are sometimes, literally, acts of God or Nature. It forces every player, even the best, to concede that perfection is rare.
>
> And it presents the kind of complexity that evolves from what seem like simple rules. In business, goals and principles are generally simple and even painfully obvious: "Buy low/sell high," perhaps, or "Create sustainable competitive advantage." But as every practitioner knows, once you start trying to do that in the real world, it gets a lot more complex. Many of us find that challenge exhilarating, even worth a lifetime of our full efforts. Golf, it turns out, is the same way. And that's apparently what makes it so addictive.

same feelings, whether they are saving lives or chasing frisbees; to them, it's all play. (Maybe *that's* why they're required in the White House, to offset all that West Wing weightiness.) The implication is obvious: Work like a dog and also *play* like a dog—with abandon and selflessness.

When it comes to the link between fun and full engagement, the bottom line is simple: We're told that two-thirds of workers don't like their jobs and feel no sense of commitment to the organization. If your workers are having fun, if you can help them get that feeling we all get when we're fully engaged, when work feels like play, will your team's performance be merely average? Of course not—you'll be much more like the great first-wave companies that were built around a culture of purposeful but genuine play. Companies like Ford, Apple, Yahoo, HP, Nokia, JP Morgan...and DoCoMo.

No Fun, No Play, No Innovation

Probably the most important reason to have fun is this: *Fun drives innovation.*

Making sure that you have innovation, of course, is Very Serious Business. In an era of rapid change (and if this era isn't, what is?), innovation becomes a required core capability. No matter what business you are in, you (and your competitors) have all the ingredients needed for innovation: underlying technological advances, cheap capital, a free flow of know-how within and between industries, and acceptance from Wall Street to Main Street that everything is going to change. In times like these, if you're not part of the innovation steamroller, you absolutely will become part of the road.

And even when innovation isn't required by the times, it is one of the very few ways that you can build sustainable competitive advantage. Unless you innovate, you are simply delivering a conventional product, using a conventional process to get there. That means you have only one way to compete: to become ever more efficient or effective. A noble goal...but tiring. Doing the same thing as everyone else, the same way, but somehow doing it cheaper or better is certainly a narrow path—and probably a short one, as well, with an ugly final scene to be played out there at Dead End Canyon.

So managing for innovation is serious, even critical. Where's the fun in that? Simple—it's at the mysterious and unavoidable human heart of innovation itself. Without fun, most new ideas would never have been born. (And what would? Nature has a way of attaching pleasurable, immediate rewards to those creative endeavors that ensure the species survives.)

Let's be realistic. What we are really talking about, when we calmly discuss innovation, is a small miracle. Genius. Creativity. Invention. It's a vital part of business—heck, it's vital to life on the planet—but ultimately mysterious. That's why, for centuries, we have viewed innovators with special respect, sometimes approaching awe. It is also why innovators themselves are often mystified and superstitious about where the ideas come from. From inside or outside, we *know* that innovation requires just the right human touch. You can't always define what is needed, but when it's there (or missing!), you can easily see the results. No matter how you slice it, that's pretty mysterious.

Innovation is a small miracle. It's a

vital part of business—heck, it's vital to life on

the planet—but ultimately mysterious.

We haven't solved the mystery—we're not sure it *can* be solved, or should be. But we do observe, in experiences at DoCoMo and all kinds of other places, that fun and innovation are almost impossible to untangle.

Skeptical again? Don't take our word for it, or DoCoMo's; just look to your own experience. This time, think about the last really great idea you came up with. Now ask yourself these questions:

- The thinking that produced the idea—the process that was happening in your head—was it the kind of orderly, analytical, directed thinking we use to get through most of each day?

- Could you comfortably put that thought process on a flow diagram, or write it into a proposal, or try to manage other people doing it? Or did your great idea just seem to appear, either popping in completely at random, or caroming off some unlikely subject?

- At the moment the idea appeared, were you tense, or relaxed?

- Were you perhaps even doing something that occupies some of your attention—but not much—shaving, taking a shower, hiking a familiar trail?

There's a reason that kind of thing happens, to all of us.

Moment of Truth #3
Great Ideas, Meet My Company

For a real eye-opener, though, stop thinking about those pleasant moments when innovation works. Shift your focus, instead, to a painful moment of truth: the first time you learned that innovation and corporate life don't naturally mix.

Brainstorming or Barnstorming

Maybe it was a mandatory brainstorming session. You could tell this was no ordinary staff meeting, because there were big sheets of paper tacked up on the wall, colorful markers everywhere, and a stern injunction that "there are no bad ideas here today." Despite these intentions, the *feel* of a staff meeting was there. All eyes remained on the boss; you felt a vague sense that everything you would hear had been said before, probably by the same people—*déjà vu* without the thrill; and the space/time continuum did one of those strange, Einsteinian loops where thousands of painful seconds ticked away while the clock barely moved at all.

When the "let's brainstorm" speech had droned to a close, the silence was deafening. You could almost see the empty thought bubbles over everyone's heads, like the cartoonist had forgotten to add the joke. People who *always* have something to say found fascinating things to inspect on their notepads. Even your own mind suddenly felt a lot less crowded—almost lonely. And the ideas that did make it out seemed...not just ordinary, but (forgive us)...stupid. In the end, you all survived. Most people said something—anything. Those huge sheets of paper got filled. But it all felt a lot less creative than you'd imagined. Worst of all, outside the room, where the great ideas were supposed to matter, nothing really changed.

Sharing Yourself

Or maybe this moment of truth came when you were sharing one of your own innovations, a great one, with customers, senior execs, or venture capitalists. Before your very eyes, people who had sworn they wanted "out-of-the-box thinking" turned into the most obsessive box builders you'd ever seen—connoisseurs of containment. Self-styled captains of industry suddenly became passionate followers of the business herd, preferably way, way in the back. Investors who once waxed poetic about risk/reward and 10-baggers showed new interest in T-bills. All the predictable objections, things you'd worked around long before, didn't just come up; they bogged down discussion for what seemed like hours. And the unpredictable objections, real wack jobs, came not only from left field but from everywhere else. Maybe you even heard, from the same people who'd begged for innovation, "great ideas are a dime a dozen. It's execution that matters."

If you've been in those painful, idea-killing rooms, you're not alone. Not because so many people in business are imperfect (though we are). But because these moments of torture flow directly from the great truths about innovation:

- When you are doing anything new, no matter how brilliant, you will be amazed by the resistance you meet.

- Creating anything new and worthwhile is hard.

- Real innovation is a mysterious process that calls on the deepest parts of ourselves.

- The process just plain hurts.

A Long Shot

Think about what you're asking of your team, when you demand innovation (and whether you pass the message on or not, the market is ALWAYS demanding it). This is an experimental, long-shot process. Most new ideas don't make it. So you need to generate the right assortment of options. You need a big range, because success is unpredictable. But you can't generate them all—there are too many logical possibilities to even write them all down, much less act on them. So you and your people need the creativity and insight to see, invent, or find the unpredictable set of options that will get you where you're going.

But that's just for openers. Then you need to go from this big set of options to a short list that you can research, develop, and test. Someone needs the very special instinct to screen out the right ones but let through some that don't make sense, on paper, but will make it in the market. The idea of trying screensavers as an early mobile application, for instance: in retrospect, it may seem obvious...but who would have thought?

Even at this screening stage, creativity and wildness are absolutely necessary. If all you do is put your best and smartest people to the task of making good screening decisions, you'll end up doing to your innovation effort what peer review does to science—holding back the new approach until there's *lots* of evidence it might work. In science, there are arguably good reasons for that conservative bias. And there is an explicitly studied mechanism for overcoming it; that's where the phrase "paradigm shift" came from. But business, you will have noticed, moves faster than science. You need to cultivate gut instincts, somewhere, to let the right long shots through.

Placing Bets

Finally, someone has to decide where to place your bet (if you're lucky, you might even get to place two or three). Looking at your "short list of long shots," someone has to pick the lucky winner(s) to be launched, or at least pilot tested. Even with all the market research in the world, this is ultimately a judgment call, especially in areas where the technology, idea, or product is so new that no one, not even the consumer herself, really knows what she wants.

FIGURE 5-2. Most new ideas don't make it.

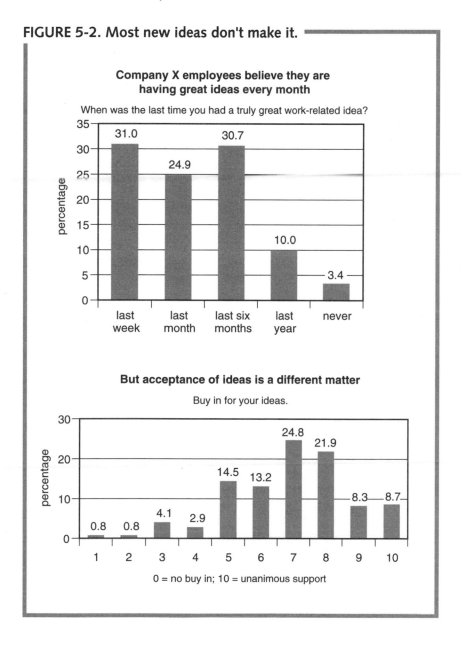

Back in the early 1980s, when personal computers were first coming to the attention of fairly normal people, the big question was "what's this thing for?" (Wireless data faced exactly the same question in Japan about three years ago and faces it now in the United States and much of Europe.) There were a few common answers that people tried over and over again. These answers, like "balancing your checkbook" and "organizing your recipes" might have been used to rationalize a few computer sales, but it's hard to believe they every really drove a single computer purchase. (Even today, Quicken and Microsoft Money are great tools. But on a strict cost/benefit basis, would they really justify the full cost of a computer, the space to put it, the continuing software upgrades, and the user's time in training and system maintenance?)

There were also real killer apps that evolved, sweeping millions of new buyers into the market; we've already mentioned the classic example, VisiCalc. Of course, the people who bought PCs for VisiCalc didn't all end up using spreadsheets most of the time; once the technology was in place, they began to experiment with it or learn from colleagues who were experimenting. But by then, the question "what's this thing for?" was no longer a survival issue. For new market entrants, of course, new answers were needed. The right answer, for a while, was desktop publishing; then it was e-mail; then it was the Web. Now it's shifting again, to whatever turns out to really drive the mobile device market.

The point here isn't that experts are wrong—though that can be entertaining. The point is that technology and technology use evolve together, quickly and under multiple influences. So no one can predict very far out. Yet we all have to make bets. The only way to see what technology can do for your business, or which technologies will survive, is to let them compete in the actual market. (It has to be the real market, not one we simulate, because the simulation can only have in it what we know or believe. And by definition this is an area where knowledge and beliefs are on very shaky ground. If market research and smart modeling really worked with any precision, would Motorola and other investors have spent $5 billion on Iridium? Would

EMI have agreed to pay Mariah Carey a $20 million advance for one album? In this kind of world, when it's time to place a bet, you need people with well-educated guts.)

Innovation isn't hard only because it's mysterious. At least half the challenge is that innovation forces you to confront real, major risks. In the end, business innovation is, literally, a form of evolution: Lots of variations are tried, most fail, but the ones that succeed may well get to take over the whole ecosystem. As in nature, from the perspective of the ecosystem—or the winner—it's a beautiful and amazing process. (Not to mention one we can't opt out of.) But for any particular species, and certainly for any individual participant, natural selection can be really, really ugly. At that level, in fact, it is ugly for most players most of the time. No matter who you are, in what industry or setting, betting on any given innovation is a low-percentage play.

Hate the Loss, but Not the Loser

And low-percentage plays do not fit comfortably into our analytic and organizational processes (the ones that are practically invisible to us, they are so much part of our culture). They *really* don't fit with our emotions. Nobody likes to fail at anything. When the stakes are real, nobody wants to even hear about true long-shot investments, the kind where you might make a huge pile of money but are more likely to lose it all. Lottery tickets prove the point; millions of people buy those because the stakes seem low: They're risking what they see as throw-away money, even a single dollar at a time, for the (infinitesimally small but oh so exciting) chance of winning life-changing money.

At the other end of the scale, 401Ks teach the same lesson. Most investment is in what are perceived to be the safest investment choices—either the ones that are mathematically conservative, like guaranteed investment contracts, or the ones that feel safe because they are in a familiar, solid company—your own. (We've become numb to those Enron losses. But remember, individual human beings were actually counting on that stock to fund their retirement. They thought they were doing the right thing.) When we do lose visible money in an investment, any investment, it doesn't just feel unfortunate; it feels, well...unfair. Life is not supposed to be that way.

It is risk, or more precisely, our fear of risk, that makes so much attempted innovation painful and ultimately fruitless. The fears are everywhere: in our heads, our organizations, our customers, and our critics (who are present, in this media-saturated age, in every setting). No one wants to lose. Missing out on a potential win, on the other hand, saying no to what would have been the opportunity of a lifetime, is far less painful. After all, we so seldom know, for sure, that it would have worked out. But when you lose money, you can see, *that* is undeniable.

We humans are, quite sensibly, wired to avoid danger. Over thousands of generations, we have evolved to be innovators—yet to be deeply, deeply skeptical of the unknown. That's what makes those brainstorming sessions so painful, and potential allies so skeptical. The mind is doing its job, telling us that it's OK to take this risk. In fact, if we don't take it, we're more likely to lose. But the heart, or maybe the part of the brain that evolved way before risk/benefit calculus, knows better. It's never time to take a risk. The odds are against us. And it feels like physical survival is at stake.

What Fun Will Do for You

Here's where things get fun—or have to, if we're ever going to overcome our deep *feelings* about risk and therefore actually try new ideas. To overcome our emotionally based barriers to innovation, we need an emotionally based incentive: fun.

■ *Fun outweighs fear.* DoCoMo's leaders understood that equation. That is why they invested in Club Mari, in playful off-site meetings, and in all kinds of activity that could have brought them to shame in this most shame-conscious culture. They did it under the gun. To survive, they had to invent a great new product, and the business built around it. They needed innovation, and fast. So they invested in fun.

Five years, and 16 trillion yen in revenues later, DoCoMo is still counting on the same equation. Many of the issues surrounding 3G (the advanced mobile capabilities rolling out now in Japan—and in a year or two elsewhere) are, at their core, technical problems. The same is true for 4G—which the Japanese are already pursuing in earnest. So visits there showed DoCoMo busily making sure engineers have plenty of fun.

■ ***Fun takes learning to the next level.*** Fun is more than just a bribe or anesthetic for people who need to take risks (like you). It's also a way of letting your mind really do its stuff. Creating something new always has an element of learning: it's discovery. That kind of learning (not memorizing, not wrapping our analytical minds around someone else's framework, but really *getting* something that no one else is trying to teach us) requires flashes of insight. Having fun encourages those irreplaceable bursts of learning. As Arie de Geus, who at Royal Dutch Shell set new standards for creative strategy, has put it: "Play is the most rare and potentially the most powerful [form of learning]."

When we're having fun, we tend to use "fluid intelligence," not "crystallized intelligence." Fluid intelligence is what babies use. For them, the world is not set in stone; there is not a formula for everything. It is all about trial and error, and the whole world is a big amusement park while those synapses are being formed. Once they are formed, we can call them in a "crystallized" way to help us with our decision making. Normally functioning adults don't have any problem with crystallized intelligence—it is almost coming out of our ears. But we do need to inject some fun-building fluid intelligence opportunities into our lives. When we do, we find ourselves able to look at problems from different angles, even to take on the viewpoint of another person. When you're trying to innovate in ways that will create value for customers, knowing how they look at the world—really seeing it the same way—is crucial. Remember Mari's concierge insight? After all, Alan Kay, called by some the father of personal computing, claimed that point of view is worth fifty IQ points.

■ ***Fun gives us access to the subconscious.*** Innovation calls for more than risk and learning; it also calls for several kinds of *thinking* processes that, to be honest, don't sound like thinking at all. There are those flashes of insight. Think about the times when, even though you know you should be doing the departmental budget or finishing that memo, you find yourself doodling on a pad—and suddenly the rough sketch appears that reframes the organizational problem you need to fix. Those moments don't last long, but they can be priceless.

And there are ideas that simply must come from visions—something in the mind that sounds a lot more like feeling than like thought. When Tachikawa first argued that 3G, with its "always on" nature, created the potential for five times as many mobile devices in Japan as there are people—the extras going to pets and appliances—it's hard to see that coming out of any really cognitive process. This is the sub conscious getting its voice out there—and it is critical to any creative act. A steady diet, of course, would be exhausting. It might not be possible. And it certainly would limit your options in most businesses we know about. But a little more bandwidth between our business selves and our subconscious minds would be a very good thing. We can't think of a better way to get there than having more fun.

■ *Fun brings freedom and spontaneity.* Innovation requires us to break out of predictable variables, established ranges, and well-worn combinations. That's a very good recipe for fun, as well. The root of much humor is putting something familiar into an unusual context. That can't happen if you're criticizing your thoughts as you go, or even trying to direct them. When you're not in play mode, great ideas don't occur to you; you edit them out, without even knowing that you are doing it.

The well-worn "no bad ideas" rule for group brainstorming is fine as far as it goes. But it doesn't go far enough. It's the editing that happens beneath the surface of each person's brain, not in the room, that is deadliest. Getting into a playful mode is a great way of turning the internal editor and manager off.

■ *Fun helps us to connect to others.* If you want to innovate, get some new ideas. Such cross-fertilization of ideas doesn't require contact with another human being; you can read or watch TV. But good ideas often spring from interaction with friends and colleagues. The whole reason for think tanks like Accenture's Institute for Strategic Change or Mitch's former employer, RAND, is to put a bunch of bright people in the same place together, focused on the most important problems, and hope that innovative thinking emerges. In today's wired and wireless world, these kinds of interactions can be electronic. But they will be much more effective if there is an element of fun in the electronic communication.

One of the i-mode users whom we interviewed described his interaction with friends this way: "We keep in contact by sending silly [text] messages...we can be closer to our friends." Sometimes this silliness turns into great new ideas, sometimes it is just silliness, but both have an important place.

Taking the Fun Out of Innovation

If all this talk of fun, play, and spontaneity sounds like New Age pabulum, let us suggest three experiments. Any one of them will give you a persuasive, clinical view of unplayful, unspontaneous, unfun innovation.

1. *Read some computer-generated writing.* There's a long tradition of seeing whether, given the right rules and word lists, computers can create poetry, fiction, etc. One of our favorite examples, recounted at book length by the computer scientist involved, was "teaching" a computer to generate folktales. The experiment began with an already-constructed "grammar" of the tales, and the author thought that automating the process would take perhaps a few days. It ended up consuming years and demonstrating (in our view) that even powerful computers programmed by very smart people with the benefit of generations of literary analysis cannot successfully do what Russian peasants did in their spare time.

2. *Talk with Eliza.* You've probably met this machine-based therapist, or at least heard of her. Eliza was running on university mainframes and CPM machines not long after Bill Gates dropped out of

Box 5-4. A session with Eliza.

Eliza: Hello. How do you do. Please state your problem.

Patient: My problem is too much work.

Eliza: Your problem is too much work?

Patient: Yes, I have too much to do.

Eliza: You seem to be quite positive.

Patient: I am positive that I have too much to do.

Eliza: Is it because you are positive that you have too much to do that you came to me?

Patient: Yes, that is why I came to you.

Eliza: You are sure.

Patient: Absolutely.

Eliza: But your problem is too much work .

Patient: Indeed.

Eliza: I'm not sure I understand you fully.

Patient: I think not.

Eliza: You say you think not?

Patient: Yes, I think you don't understand me.

Eliza: I see.

Patient: Can you help me?

Eliza: You believe I can help you, don't you?

Patient: No.

Eliza: Are you saying no just to be negative?

Patient: No.

Eliza: You are being a bit negative.

Harvard, so she doesn't represent the state of artificial intelligence. What she does is simulate a conversation with a Rogerian therapist—you know, the "how do you feel about (whatever subject you just mentioned)" routine. Eliza is hilarious at first and can even be scary for brief periods. Box 5-4 contains an excerpt from an actual "conversation," or you can try her for yourself at several Web sites, including *http://chayden.net/eliza/Eliza.shtml*. But (besides the power of a well-organized verbal routine), what she demonstrates, if you use her for long, is that even very predictable human conversations have a lot of meaning that analyzed and constructed ones do not. A conversation with Eliza or her succesors might pass the Turing test—you might be fooled into thinking you were interacting with a human being—but it will not change how you feel about the world.

3. *Watch some mediocre TV.* One cognitive scientist and programming prodigy of our acquaintance has suggested that the vast majority of TV and movie scripts are, in fact, generated by AI programs. He's kidding, sort of. He knows that these shows are written by hip, intelligent, well-paid people. But, being a provocateur, he would argue that the people grinding out those forgettable works are in fact a giant, distributed, flesh-and-blood AI program. And he's making a serious point that tells us why spontaneity is crucial to real innovation.

Our friend's argument is that it is precisely the *bad* variations you would expect to come from an automated effort. Not because computers or computer scientists are inherently stupid—our friend, at least, thinks quite the opposite—but because what can be modeled and routinized (because it is NOT spontaneous) is exactly the recipe you'd follow to create works that are not very innovative: Take a formula that has worked, vary one or several of the parameters in predictable ways, and hope the audience won't see through the process. If what you need is an orderly and predictable "creative" process, then prepare yourself for mediocrity. If what your business needs is innovation, then you've got to live with some weirdness. How better to get weird, without real danger, than by having fun?

Moment of Truth #4
Paying More Than You Need to Pay—
and Liking It

As important as fun is *inside* your team, there is another place where it's probably even more vital: in your product, service, and advertising. Providing genuine, personal fun is one of the best ways of delivering real value to the customer—way more important than most buyers will ever let on. And for any product trying to get through the killer-app stage, fun can be a lifesaver. It certainly was for DoCoMo; the earliest i-mode applications, the ones that seemed to drive Japanese buyers to purchase the right equipment and actually use the data service, were fun. We mean not only the screensavers and ringtones, which have gotten so much press, but e-mail, as well.

The bottom line is simple: Innovation comes

from someplace beyond the reach of our flow

diagrams and process manuals. Getting to that

place requires some process that typically

doesn't look manageable, or even productive.

In our experience, and in DoCoMo's history,

fun is the best way of getting there.

E-mail certainly has a nonfun side, or at least it does for most of us. But it has been the killer app for many a corporate information system, precisely because it almost always brings new opportunities for human connectedness, to say nothing of novelty. All that communication can be justified in cost/benefit terms, but, in real life, it's often about fun. Using e-mail on an entirely new, mobile device boosts the fun quotient considerably. Who hasn't received, or sent, one of those e-mails whose only real purpose is to share with others the new user's joy at being able to e-mail from an airplane on the tamarc? Another fun aspect, individualizing i-mode phones with accessories, quickly became a huge industry. But is the fun that DoCoMo delivered to its customers, on its way to market domination, unique? Or could fun matter to your customers as well?

Buyers Just Wanna Have Fun

To decide, consider a final, very personal, moment of truth: the last time you pretty much said "money is no object." We know, you'd never be so frivolous. But haven't you made a purchase where you not only knew you could have bought something roughly comparable for less—but didn't even consider it? We thought so. And there's a lesson in that (though it's probably not the one you're expecting).

So think about the last purchase you made where you were happy to pay a clear premium for the thing you bought. No matter what the product was, that's an important kind of purchase. Important to you, of course, because you were getting what you wanted, maybe even needed. But really important to the manufacturer, because your behavior suggests that they have a nice, profitable strategic position. Your behavior tells them that this product is (at least for you) the opposite of a commodity. It might even be a monopoly of sorts. So the manufacturer is not only making a nice margin, but can probably count on you to choose them again and even to recommend them to others.

Now think about the product itself and the feelings that were driving your decision. We're willing to bet that fun was somewhere in the mix.

Going Clubbing

Maybe the product itself is inherently fun. Golfers, for example, will shop tirelessly for new equipment; they're likely to do lots of research,

Box 5-5. ATTENTION!

A useful way to analyze the blend of fun and practical value is in terms of attention. After all, in attempting to launch a new product, the scarcest resource you are fighting for, by far, is the attention of potential customers to notice that it exists, consider it, purchase it, actually use the thing, and tell others about it. And you need many of your initial customers to do all that within, as we've said, a fairly short window.

As it happens, analyzing attention problems is something one of us knows about. John and his colleague at Accenture's Institute for Strategic Change, Tom Davenport, wrote a whole book, *The Attention Economy*, which coaches managers on how to navigate in this strange new world, where attention is more valuable than money, physical resources, or even technology. One tool John and Tom developed is the AttentionScape, which allows the user to quantify and categorize human attention.

On reaching customers with fun, the AttentionScape reveals this: There are six types of attention, in three pairs (Attractive/Aversive, Captive/Voluntary, Front of Mind/Back of Mind). To change people's behavior, it is extremely helpful to have a significant share of all six types. But fun is associated with only three: Attractive, Voluntary, and Front of Mind. To really make buyers move, you need a complement that attracts the three opposite kinds.

As John and Tom explain it to less sophisticated audiences, you want plenty of carrot, but you also need some stick. Most companies, of course, err on the side of the stick—especially in recessionary times, when layoffs are always an option. ("We're giving them a job, they should do what they are paid to do. What more do they want?") If you've made it this far in the Fun chapter, you know that DoCoMo and we disagree.

But we also disagree with those who try to capture attention through fun alone. It works for a while, but Tom and John's research showed that you get more attention (and sales) when the flip side of all of the attention types is involved. Think of it this way: A trip to Disneyland is pure fun. Yet the appeal is also, always, partly about risk: "If you don't come to Disneyland, you'll be missing out on the fun that all of your friends are having." Video games are fun, but the ones that sell best are those where so many of your friends have the game that you can't afford not to be there too.

including trial and error; to poll their friends; to read everything in sight. They may well look hard for the best price on their equipment of choice. But what they won't do, despite strong suggestions from significant others or even their own normally thrifty better judgment, is choose any club except *the exact one they want*. If the driver they feel best about is $375, and one nearly as good is $300, very few golfers will settle for second best. That's a 25 percent premium! The same thing is true, for many buyers, for shoes and clothing: Any marketer knows that if you can create an emotional connection between the buyer and your product, price becomes much less important. But their usual tool for that is advertising. And although the emotions stirred up by a great ad can be powerful, their half-life is equally short, unless they are truly intrinsic to the product itself.

What you really want is an emotional pull that may begin with advertising, but that gets stronger when the buyer is considering the purchase, and even stronger after the purchase is made. That's the kind of thing that builds company cults, like for Harley Davidson, where "brand equity" is a very serious asset.[5] Fun is one of the easiest connections to make; look at Starbucks, for instance.

Fun is especially vital in luring buyers into an unfamiliar marketplace. In other words, fun is a great candidate for selling any killer app. Think about a product like desktop publishing. Most of us don't do anything like desktop publishing today. But in the mid 1980s, with the launch of PageMaker and the Macintosh, everyone's uncle, aunt, and cousin were suddenly putting out a weekly newsletter about the comings and goings of all their kin. It was a fun process, you could play with fonts and clip art, and when you were done, it looked like something that previously would have taken weeks of work and hundreds of dollars to produce.

When you've got a new kind of product, having the killer app isn't just critical; it's *time*-critical. Even if your company has the resources to keep pushing a product that hasn't caught on, there is a definite window of opportunity, one that closes quickly when a product has been around in people's awareness, yet hasn't caught fire. It begins to feel a little shopworn. It appears that if a new generation of technology doesn't reach a tipping point fairly soon after introduction, it may well be dead forever. Look at the promise of "500 channels of cable." Everybody, literally everybody, knew it was coming. Even Bruce Springsteen got into the act. But somehow most people didn't find that compelling (the channels, not the Boss). Cable missed the window, allowing satellite systems—which arguably offer just about the same package—to build a very important foothold in the U.S. premium TV market.

If you want to make it through the window while it's open, rather than sliding down the closed pane like the battered cat in Tom and Jerry cartoons, DoCoMo's record suggests that you build fun into your package. It can be whimsy (like i-mode's screensavers), entertainment (like the constant novelty of ringtones), social bonding (like e-mail, or i-mode fashion accessories), or personal freedom (like the exhilaration Yasuko experienced being able to conduct private conversations while living at home). But it pretty much has to be there.

Yet DoCoMo's record also illustrates that fun alone is seldom enough. Even the least serious killer apps, screensavers, and ringtones had practical value. Once the phones became popular enough in the early-adopter cliques that everyone had them, there had to be some way of identifying which phone was whose. That critical first wave of customers bought phone straps, screensavers, and ringtones not only because they were fun, but because they were practical and (almost immediately) because you needed those accessories to be part of the group. In a psychological paradox truly worthy of the Japanese, DoCoMo's buyers spent money to make their phones stand out so that they themselves would fit in.

Calling Mary Poppins

From the consumer's point of view, the blend of fun and nonfun rationales for a new product is completely natural. The buyer is looking for "rational" value to justify the price of any purchase. So you have to deliver that, almost as a price of entry. And unless your product category happens to be toys or entertainment, fun alone won't cut it. But what consumers may not be aware of, and what too many businesses overlook, is that the rational value they *think* they are after is only part of the story. You need a dose of fun, too. It's Mary Poppins' spoonful-of-sugar approach; "serious" value gives them permission to buy, then fun gets them over the hump of actually trying something new.

With i-mode, the blend was the practical value of a concierge and productive e-mail; fashion accessories, ringtones, and the fun of "chatting" with friends provided a BIG spoonful of sugar. Looking at the wireless data market in Europe and North America, it seems that without the sugar, even great mobile services go nowhere.

Till Daddy Takes the T-bird Away?

DoCoMo is far from the only company to have used this strategy. (Southwest Airlines, for instance, actually hires, promotes, and rewards staff based on their sense of humor. Flight attendants have been known to hide in the overhead bins and frequently make singing safety announcements. Even the jaded, high-mileage flyer appreciates hearing someone official send up those FAA-mandated warnings: "And for those who haven't been in a car since 1964, here is how the seatbelts work." Is it worth as much as frequent flyer miles? No, but then again, everybody offers miles; no other airline provides that kind of fun. As Southwest's financial results consistently demonstrate, the fun pays off.) But DoCoMo is certainly a leader in providing fun to customers in a traditionally utililitarian category. And it believes so heavily in fun that it's going to make it an even bigger part of i-mode's future: 3G and, beyond it, 4G.

With 3G, DoCoMo is facing the same problem that every wireless carrier confronts (or will, someday): what is all that bandwidth *for?* You will notice that this is basically a more emphatic version of the question wireless data vendors have had trouble with worldwide—except for DoCoMo. And over a couple of years of talking to experts around the world about this issue, we have found a remarkably short list of potential killer apps for 3G.

DoCoMo is certainly aware of the problem. Its response is to up the ante...on fun. If i-mode was a concierge with a little fun thrown in, 3G is more like a stand-up comic that happens to do errands.

The best way to see the emphasis on fun is to look closely at the company's visions for the future. Most of NTT DoCoMo's hopes for the killer apps of the future are contained in a video, "2010 Vision," available on NTT DoCoMo's Web page. For full-bandwidth fans (like us— we can imagine "too rich and too thin," but too much bandwidth is like "faster than lightspeed," the stuff of physics and science fiction), the vision can also be shared on a visit to the DoCoMo showroom. This scenario is presented as a story of one Japanese family. The first installment, set in 2003, shows applications for current 3G phones: video conversations, home appliance networks, shopping information, educational communication, downloading music, vending machine transactions, sending photographs, and database access. There's plenty of fun.

But where things really get interesting is in the second phase, when we are transported to 2010. By now, the son is in high school—attending classes in virtual 3D while lounging in a meadow. Later, on a trip

Box 5-6. So what is 3G?

We have to apologize. Through most of this book, we've followed the lead of the wireless industry generally—referring often to 3G, but not really talking about what it is. And you've been so patient about that. Could it be that you are, like most Western customers, unsure what all this stuff is good for?

Your instincts may be right—though we have a few ideas for making mobile data so compelling you won't want to do without it. But that's another book.

Till then, for the record, here are the 3G basics. Third-generation wireless (3G) is simply a radio communication technology for transmitting voice and data at high speeds to mobile devices. The 3G Newsroom Web site defines it more specifically as the "improvements in wireless data and voice communications through any of a variety of proposed standards. The immediate goal is to raise transmission speeds from 9.5K to 2M bit/sec."

According to UMTS, 3G will mean the following things:

- Enhanced multimedia (voice, data, video, remote control)

- Usability on all popular modes (cellular telephone, e-mail, paging, fax, videoconferencing, and Web browsing)

- Broad bandwidth and high speed (upward of 2 Mbps)

- Routing flexibility (repeater, satellite, LAN)

- Operation at approximately 2 GHz transmit and receive frequencies

- Roaming capability throughout Europe, Japan, North America

to Bangkok, the now-retired husband takes virtual golf lessons while standing on the porch of his traditional Thai-style bungalow. The daughter is getting married, in Paris, of course, and although grandma can't attend in person, her lifesize virtual self is there, standing right next to the aisle.

By now, you're probably shaking your head. We've seen many of these future scenarios, good and bad, and the head shaking always starts sometime. It's the nature of trying to predict the future, especially for an audience of jaded twenty-first century info-tech types. Even the youngest manager has seen so many unexpected things happen and so many Buck Rogers visions fail to appear. Yet there is no alternative; everyone in the wireless data market is playing the futurism game.

DoCoMo's vision, though, is different. It's not the only vision we like; there are good ideas in several other places, and some we can't discuss yet. And it has its share of moments that leave us shaking our heads, as well. But we see more fun in DoCoMo's vision—fun seems to be at the very core of its projected experience. When future becomes present and these advanced applications hit the market, the fun factor could well make the difference; it certainly did for i-mode.

Showroom Fun

And the fun isn't just in DoCoMo's public statements. It starts right at the top of the corporation and extends well into the lab where techies are literally building future apps. Let us show you.

If you are an esteemed guest, with some luck and quite a bit of advance planning, you step out of the elevator onto the twenty-ninth floor of DoCoMo's headquarters in Tokyo, walk into a tasteful waiting area, and meet a pair of "tour guides" who look like they just came from an Issey Miyake runway and who, of course, speak flawless English. In twenty years of doing business in Japan, these are the tallest Japanese women John has ever encountered—probably 5' 11" not counting the obligatory heels.

These women, carefully chosen to reflect DoCoMo's vision of the future, lead visitors to what is, underneath it all, a playroom for adults. Everything is very tasteful, and the goal of serious business is always there—this is an elite presentation. But it's all about the pure fun of gadgets, advanced technology that can do amazing things. And the demonstrations are all about fun. One guide takes a group photo, using a next-generation i-mode phone—then transmits it wirelessly to a printer across the room. Visitors have video chats with each other. The tour guides show off a detailed mock-up of a Formula One car, demonstrating how 3G technology can send video feeds and digital information back to the pit crew during a race (if only Formula One rules allowed it). You probably could think of no-nonsense applications for all these capabilities, but why would you? The feeling, of the moment and presumably of the i-mode future, is all about fun.

On a less polished visit, in the depths of DoCoMo's R&D lab, the same theme is evident. If anything, the demo room at DoCoMo's Yokosuka research facility is even less about practicality. The displays aren't as slick, but that somehow makes them even more edgy. And the fun quotient is very high. Most of these displays have been designed as games. You might find yourself behind the wheel of an arcade-quality car-racing game and, like an author who prefers to remain anonymous, come away with no clear memory of what wireless capability was in play—but with an adrenaline rush you'll never forget.

Putting Fun in Your Pocket

DoCoMo doesn't just demonstrate fun as part of its future; it believes in it. That doesn't mean they aren't developing practical applications, like field technicians transmitting pictures of damaged equipment to get quick second opinions from their coworkers back home. But the practical value isn't enough to catch attention and drive adoption. Some of it can be done today with J-Phone's picture phone, for instance, or with still pictures. DoCoMo seems to believe that delivering fun, in the deepest sense, is mandatory. Just look at a few of the applications under development.

Videophones

This is the most obvious 3G app. If your problem is excess bandwidth, video is a great way to eat it up. Videophone is also a technology that is easy to be skeptical about. You can get that shopworn, never-gonna-happen vibe; after all, the Dick Tracy watch was a dream for people who are now becoming grandparents. And there have been so many attempts that never really took off, ranging from the AT&T display at the 1964 World's Fair to its attempt to market videophones in the 1990s to Webcam and voice systems today. Even after barriers of size, bandwidth, cost, and complexity are assumed away (or transcended by technology), there is still the nagging question: "If I don't know anyone else who has one of these things, whom would I call?" Video-phones seem to be on the wrong side of network effects.

But we wouldn't count this app out. First, any kind of warm and novel personal communication, once it's easy to do, has a high fun factor. For example, look at the explosion of instant messaging. In answer to the skeptics who point out that you can often accomplish the same thing with voice or e-mail, IM users say that messaging just feels different. (And we have to admit that instant messaging goes a long way to solve the problems of virtual teams spread out all over the continent. If your buddy lists and notifications are set up correctly, messaging replaces those random water-cooler interactions that keep physical office staffs working together.)

Second, the problem of compatible hardware was a lot tougher back when people rented a landline phone for life. I-mode users are already replacing their phones every year or so, and they form a kind of built-in community. If the only people you could v-phone were other i-mode users, young people especially would find that to be just about all they need. For example, people like Yasuko and Mariko, who invest so much time in the subtleties of various relationships, would find video a real addition. And just as business people have long since learned to use conference calls as a "warmer" medium than e-mail or one-on-one phones, we can imagine i-mode business clients upgrading to 3G video-phones to, as they say, build relationships.

Alibi Software

For more outrageous fun—possibly the Bandai screensaver of the 3G set—developers are hard at work on "alibi software." While reporting back from an overseas trip, on videophone, you could superimpose the backdrop of a hotel business center to hide the fact that you are actually sitting in a sidewalk café or on a beach on the Riviera. Although it sounds like a joke, we know many Japanese (not to mention Westerners) who would love the idea.

Instructional Videos

At least two years before 3G launched in Tokyo, a group of Accenture consultants in Japan participated in an informal contest to see if they could come up with a killer app for 3G. The "winner" was a system for sending golfing tips and short instructional videos to a 3G phone. The idea is that golfers could call up a short video while on the course to correct a particularly debilitating hook or slice without having to stop their game. Golf, of course, is not the only application; small Japanese companies are working on short foreign language instructional videos and computer skills tutorials. But it could be a great killer app to drive initial use; nowhere is the motivation so high as when your friends are watching you spray balls all over the landscape. And you could make the call privately, while out in the rough "searching for your ball." Or share the lesson with the whole foursome; at least that might take the attention off you.

Music Downloading

Like video, music downloading is a natural way to use all that new 3G bandwidth; today's technologies make it impractical to download anything more complex or high fidelity than a ringtone. But with full-speed broadband, you'll be able to download the latest hits into your MP3-enabled phone in a minute and listen to it immediately. And the value seems to be there. We know that music can drive young people to try out new software (especially if the bandwidth is essentially free, as is the case for college students or 3G users). We know that the appetite is unlimited (20 gig jukeboxes are now quite common). And we know that music is often an impulse purchase, highly interactive with the people you are around and the setting you are in. So we can easily imagine a try-and-buy kind of business model. Nothing is certain in information technology, but this seems like a natural…and the fun angle is certainly there.

Making Fun Work for Your Business

By now you've figured out that we are zealots about fun (our colleagues will be shocked). You've seen that DoCoMo has invested heavily in fun, with great results so far. And, if you've read this far, you've decided for yourself that fun might actually be useful. If you're ready to take the plunge, or at least a little dip, what do we suggest? Four easy options.

■ *Make sure your team's environment supports innovation and high performance by adding some fun elements.* This can be a matter of high strategy—we have found war gaming especially useful. Such simulations are used by at least forty of the Fortune 100. Or you can go the Club Mari route—adjusted, of course, for your local standards. For a quick, no-risk option, institute just one fun policy to drive creativity, probably without making a big deal of it. On the executive team of the Georgia State Health Planning Agency, for instance, the last person to arrive has to chair the staff meeting. The result? Everyone gets very creative about trying to make someone else late. An object lesson that makes staff meetings go faster is what we call a win-win.

■ *Expect innovation from the organization, not just from "creatives."* Once you recognize that effective business innovation does not only come from geniuses, but also requires innovation at every stage and level, you see the need for fun to ease risk and open up creative thinking. Make sure your brainstorming sessions aren't like that moment of truth we described. Try to give everybody an opportunity to feel playful while they are working. Remember how it felt? If you make a real effort, the worst that can happen is your employees will be a little happier and a little more loyal. If they become visibly more creative…wouldn't that make it a home run?

■ *Think fun in your product—including the hidden reasons people might buy* (like talking to their boyfriends or having a really cool-looking gadget). If you don't yet have the culture to put fun into the product, invest in it. The single boldest move, with perhaps the highest payoff, is bringing in your own version of Enoki or Mari—the folks who can help bring out the fun and creativity in your whole, hard-working team.

■ *Put your heart into it.* This is the easiest, the safest, and yet probably the most important because it will lead you to see other opportunities. Over the next two weeks, take four quick actions:

1. List, privately, the three most fun times you've had in your life.

2. Find a common theme linking these fun experiences.

3. Do something in the next week, related to work if at all possible, that incorporates this theme.

4. Get your team to try the same thing.

Notes

1. Thomas J. Stanley, *The Millionaire Mind* (Kansas City: Andrews McMeel, 2000).

2. Mihaly Csikszentmihalyi, *Flow: The Psychology of Optimal Experience* (New York: HarperCollins, 1991).

3. Michael Schrage, *Serious Play: How the World's Best Companies Simulate to Innovate* (Boston: Harvard Business School Press, 1999).

4. Martha Beck, *Finding Your Own North Star* (New York: Crown Publishing, 2001).

5. See, for example, the Harley case study in Sam Hill and Glenn Rifkin, *Radical Marketing* (New York: HarperBusiness, 1999).

CHAPTER SIX

Strength

"It is excellent to have a giant's strength, but it is
tyrannous to use it like a giant."

—SHAKESPEARE

"OK," you might be saying about now. "So managing passions was a big part of DoCoMo's initial success. So it took the company to the top of a very exclusive list: the huge and lasting successes, the real corporate superpowers that emerged from the original Internet wave. So it even put DoCoMo in a position to lead not only its market, but its country. So what? What does all that mean going forward? And what does it mean for me?"

It's a fair question. DoCoMo's success to date is a great story. The young firm already has an impressive past, built by skillful and fortunate use of human passions. But that, in the end, is history. As always, you can draw lessons from it that may improve your own decisions. Ultimately, though, what matters is the future. Is DoCoMo really going to go any further? Or has it reached a plateau? Will it remain a giant only in its home market, which never seems quite comparable to the rest of the world? Or does its gift for leading through passion translate to Europe and North America?

Answering questions like that is always dangerous. No matter how sharp your insight into the past, building on it to predict the future is inherently a long shot. Most analysts hate making predictions, because they know how many factors are involved. Yet the rest of the world—the executives and managers and leaders who actually have to make decisions today, even without all the data they need—is always pressing for just such predictions.

There are, of course, two safe responses. One is to strap on the analyst's traditional armor: caveats. If you add enough conditions and qualifiers, then you can't be proven wrong. The other response is a variant on a (generally unsuccessful) anti-hacking technique called "security through obscurity." In this case, it means making a lot of predictions. There may be some statistical value in doing this: the law of large numbers is conceivably on your side. Far more important, though, is the strategic impact. First, when you make a lot of predictions, the discussion shifts from right-or-wrong to batting averages. This is much more comfortable territory. Second, if you're careful to practice this technique in some field where many people are making predictions all the time, your clinkers get lost in the noise. Everyone is so busy talking about the next big thing that no one is really paying attention to who correctly predicted the last one. Without the safety provided by this tactic, political handicapping and Wall Street commentary would be much less entertaining.

When it comes to predicting DoCoMo's future, either tactic should be tempting. As Masao Nakamura, executive vice president in charge of the mobile media division, points out, "All wireless companies have to think of other ways to grow business around the world. It can't just be voice. They all need much more. So they'll start to get into a business that we've been able to lead so far. In the next five years, the world will be more mobile than ever; e-commerce and information technology services will really become a more complex world." So DoCoMo faces serious challenges from not only the best wireless companies in the world, but also from leaders and aggressive new entrants in related fields. Convergence makes the competition tougher, and tougher to predict, than ever before. So who would be foolish enough to predict DoCoMo's future?

We would. To be fair, we're not alone in this; we're joined by everyone who decides to invest in the company (or not), to partner with them (or not), or to compete in mobile data (or not). All of us are taking a risk, no matter how we bet. Mitch and John, though, may be taking a little less risk than it appears. Why? Because we have inside information. Not the type the SEC would care about, but powerful stuff all the same. We know the emotional base that DoCoMo's future is built on. And, in our view, it's very strong indeed.

In fact, the central passion that will propel DoCoMo during this next phase is strength itself. Or, more precisely, the feeling of strength. Not the naive and arrogant confidence of a strong adolescent. Not the brittle strength of a competitor who has never really been tested. Not the bravado of a market leader who, entering a new phase, can't even conceive of the challenges it will face, both externally and internally. No, what we see in DoCoMo is an inner strength so quiet that many here in the West could miss it altogether.

Though understated, this strength has been proven and hardened in the firm's early days. It is not showy, not all that visible, and is certainly not aggressive. But it is very, very deep. At this juncture, DoCoMo's passionate feeling of strength is focused principally on two distinct challenges. It flows from two key leaders. And we believe that, as long as DoCoMo continues to drive from and manage this passion, the firm will reach far greater heights than competitors outside Japan would ever expect.

Challenge One, Leader One

We focus on the *feeling of* strength, not strength in objective terms, because it is that feeling that enables DoCoMo to embrace and execute strategies that many companies simply could not. On paper, DoCoMo's overall strategy is both simple and widely understood. It's an almost linear evolution that goes something like this:

analog → digital → data → IPO → video → international

Look how easy that is. It makes sense. It's the kind of plan that any MBA could draw on a white board and expand on at length. Yet, even if given the resources DoCoMo has, not one company, not one leadership team in a hundred could make it work. If they could, then DoCoMo's stellar rise would seem ordinary (after all, the first two-thirds of that whiteboard sequence have already been completed). Look at those first four steps. Back in 1995, when DoCoMo first began to understand that sequence, when its analysis suggested that the voice market would be saturated soon, a whole bunch of MBAs, inside and outside the industry, had comparable information. But DoCoMo somehow identified the need to leap from voice to data earlier than most. Much more important, it made it really work.

Having read this book, you know that a lot was involved behind the scenes, everything from love to luck, with some passions in there that no one could ever predict. But one passion that was absolutely required was an inner feeling of strength. At crucial junctures, that feeling let DoCoMo leaders learn fast and, by admitting mistakes, it let them become great partners in an industry where partnership (as they recognized earlier than others) pays incredible rewards. Without that simple, mysterious feeling of strength, DoCoMo could never have executed the first four blocks of its simple whiteboard strategy, the steps that brought it this far. The final two steps, as we will explain, are by far the hardest. Yet we expect it to succeed, precisely because DoCoMo still has, from the key leaders on down, that feeling of strength.

Whether DoCoMo still has the feeling or not, looking closely at the whiteboard strategy will tell you it is certainly going to need it. Like so many nice, linear diagrams, this one is just a bit misleading; DoCoMo doesn't really get to conquer video first, then go global. It has to succeed at the "video" stage (that is, creating real value out of the bandwidth provided by 3G). It has to go global. And it has to do both of those things, well, *starting now*. Each task is a serious challenge, for any company, anywhere. And DoCoMo's leaders will tell you candidly that at least one of them, going global, is fraught with uncertainty and fear.

Fear Begets Strength

It's strange, at first, to think that a now-giant corporation, which has never known anything but success, would even think about the emotion of fear. (Often, it seems, hot firms have just the opposite reaction; nothing scares them. Investors, afterwards, often wish that something had.) But in this case, fear makes perfect sense. To begin with, the last and longest leap, by far the most frightening, is compulsory. According to Yoshinori Uda, senior executive vice president overseeing global business, there are two reasons for DoCoMo to go international. "First, we want Japanese customers to be able to use DoCoMo services wherever they go. They should be able to carry their own i-mode phone, which they can't do now. Second, we want people around the world to be able to use i-mode services delivered by local providers."

That may not sound like compulsion; no one is holding a gun to DoCoMo's head. But think about what happens if it *doesn't* make this leap. If DoCoMo doesn't meet the simple market needs that Uda has outlined, someone else eventually will. And whoever that competitor is, wherever it is based, it will have put DoCoMo in a tough defensive position. At the very least, its market size will be tightly capped. In all probability, it'll also have to face sharper competition at home. So going global is not really a matter of choice.

And, though we in the West tend to overlook this, seeing as we do mainly their successful exports, Japanese firms are well aware of how dangerous globalization can be. Even DoCoMo, young as it is, has made some sizable missteps. The firm's first overseas investment, for example, was acquiring a chunk of Hong Kong–based Hutchison Telephone Co., Ltd. (HTCL). When the agreements were first being hammered out, DoCoMo relied heavily on its investment bankers to make sure that the complex, international agreements were sound. And from a financial perspective—which is of course what investment bankers are supposed to provide—the contracts were entirely appropriate. They protected DoCoMo in every way. But the agreements didn't necessarily take into account some important business considerations. DoCoMo's foreign partners were allowed, by contract, to bring in their own content providers and hardware manufacturers. Allowing new partners means investing more time in getting the partners up to speed. As a result, the process of getting a new system to market, DoCoMo's first attempt outside Japan, was slowed down.

This certainly wasn't a disaster. And there is no way to expect that either party should have anticipated this as a particular issue in the first place. If DoCoMo had tried to envision every potential problem before moving overseas, it would have been paralyzed by fear. Still, the timing was tough; in a new and somewhat intimidating game, it's nice to get a win under your belt before meeting the tough problems.

And this wasn't DoCoMo's only foreign misadventure. The company invested 100 billion yen (more than $3 billion U.S.) in KPN Mobile, and eventually had to write down 300 billion yen of that. Again, it was a learning experience, probably even a necessary one. (As DoCoMo's Kiyoyuki Tsujimura says, in this case "reality is not as favorable as the theory.") But anyone facing these experiences would conclude that the outside world is a seriously dangerous place.

DoCoMo absolutely shares that perception. Yet it has refused to let the vagaries of the international market keep it from making mistakes—not only these initial ones, but the others that are sure to follow. This is crucial to making globalization work, of course. And it's exactly where the *feeling of strength* comes in.

Stormy Weather

"It's a very rough sea outside Japan—very rough."

Not a surprising statement from the average Japanese citizen. Quintessential islanders, the Japanese have always been faulted for their seeming unwillingness to mingle with other nationalities—and their "stickiness" to other Japanese. Tour groups from Japan really do follow their Japanese-speaking, flag-toting guides in tight little packs. Japanese executives abroad really are known to spend a lot more time hanging out with other executives from their homeland than mingling with the local populace. And during the very week when the "rough seas" statement was made, one month after the September 11 terrorist attacks in the United States, statistics showed that Japanese domestic air travel had actually *increased* slightly after the attack—while overseas travel had dropped by almost 30 percent. Many Japanese are well aware of the stereotypes about their insular behavior, and even of what it costs them. Be that as it may, though, there is one thing the hyperisland approach has always provided: safety.

So it shouldn't surprise us that a Japanese citizen, a businessman, even, might perceive the outside world as a dangerous and unpredictable ocean. But it was a jarring statement indeed, and jarringly frank, when you realize that those words come from Kiyoyuki Tsujimura, DoCoMo's head of global business. It is even more surprising when you know that Tsujimura has not only the responsibility for taking DoCoMo global, but also remarkably strong control of the English language and a long history of living and working abroad.

Raised in Osaka, Tsujimura has a background that looks like everyone else's in the top echelons at DoCoMo—success at the best schools, followed by a rapid rise through the ranks to significant positions in the firm. As a young NTT manager, he was assigned to the team that was planning the spin-off of DoCoMo from NTT. In fact, of the top executives in DoCoMo today, only Tsujimura and his colleague Shiro Tsuda were on the original committee of thirty who planned the strategy of a new, independent wireless company. As we will see, both radiate striking, yet very different, feelings of strength. By all accounts, Tsujimura demonstrated that he was the strategic thinker on that committee. His skills there resulted in an eight-year stint as DoCoMo's chief strategic planner. He was following in august footsteps: now Chairman Ohboshi had held a similar position as the head of planning at the parent company, NTT. Finally in 1999, Tsujimura took over the global business group.

It would be a mistake to let Tsujimura's "rough seas" comment mislead you. This is no shrinking violet. This is not even the typical understated but determined Japanese manager. Tsujimura is known for his outspokenness and his hard-driving nature. He has a reputation for managing in a particularly hard-nosed "Western" manner. But among all the Western and Japanese managers we've interviewed in our research careers, we've never run into anyone at this level in a corporation who has been more willing to admit to problems. Working with successful executives, you get used to seeing people minimize the negatives and emphasize the positives. Most leaders want to give the appearance of strength, both as a natural inclination and because they know that is what the rest of us want from a leader. Without that positive, sometimes optimistic vision, few efforts would move ahead.

What Tsujimura displays is a kind of leadership that requires even greater strength: the strength to make mistakes, to admit them, and then to learn from them, not just personally but at the level of the company. After twenty years of both analyzing and experiencing the challenges of globalization, John believes that this strength is probably the single most important attribute for a businessperson operating outside his or her home country. In his experience this is a bumpy ride for everyone; it's only successful for those who learn from the bumps—and fast. Once a particular path has proven difficult or untenable, the strength and wisdom gained from making those mistakes *and acknowledging them quickly* becomes a vital advantage in international operations.

DoCoMo has that advantage, in great supply, through Tsujimura. All of us try to learn from tough experience, but struggle with barriers of pride and even our own determination; where do you draw the line between learning from your mistakes and giving up too early?

Learning from tough experience is one discipline that Tsujimura has clearly mastered. He freely admits that, as head of planning, he thought that PDAs were the way that Internet and data services would be delivered—with some kind of connection to the phone. But it turned out that PDAs were too big, too heavy, and didn't handle *kanji* well. So Tsujimura says, they tried "a Trojan horse strategy." The idea was that, since you carry a phone anyway, you might use a PDA *with* your phone. But when Enoki took control of the data services group (which later became the i-mode group), he insisted that all of the capability be put onto a cell phone alone. That changed Tsujimura's strategy completely. "Enoki was right," he says simply.

He is full of admissions of being wrong. He was wrong about PDAs; he was wrong about i-mode selling mostly to business users; he was wrong about the success of Personal Handyphone Systems (PHS). All of these mistakes were made while Tsujimura was one of the strategic planners for the company. The way that he makes these admissions so freely, without either evading or dwelling on his personal responsibility, is compelling. The way that he focuses so clearly on what the precise lessons are for DoCoMo is instructive.

Watching Tsujimura learn from his mistakes, it is easy to see why DoCoMo has been so effective at learning from its own. Like any company, DoCoMo has plenty of mistakes in its past; like any great company, it has a consistent record of moving quickly to not only cut the losses, but learn from them and move forward with renewed vigor. Surely some of that behavior comes from the powerful example set by Tsujimura and other leaders like him. And some must come from the culture, created by everyone from Ohboshi on down, which makes it possible for Tsujimura to confess his mistakes so freely. In a world where so many managers and employees describe their workgroups as "dysfunctional families," this is clearly a very functional model.

More of a Great Thing

This willingness to learn from mistakes is not only a key part of DoCoMo's past success, but an asset the firm will carry forward into the challenges of globalization. It is an asset the firm is actively leveraging through its recent IPO. As any chief executive will tell you, however many mistakes you made as a closely held company, once you go public, it will seem like you're making many more. Some CEOs see that as a burden. It must be frustrating, and it's easy to imagine that time spent "keeping the shareholders happy" is somehow at odds with time spent "actually running the business."

Yet our interviews show a different attitude within DoCoMo, one we believe flows from the same ability to admit and learn from mistakes without equivocation or delay. The feeling of strength that allows this learning to take place also allows one to learn from the criticisms of investors. Because of that feeling, the IPO and globalization of market holdings have given DoCoMo another source of strength. Masayuki Hirata, DoCoMo's chief financial officer, explains that "SEC rules are more strict than in Japan, so we have to manage more carefully than in the past…we have to be willing to talk about the risks and the negatives." Disclosure has become more important than ever. He admits that this has been a major change. In general, Hirata says, "before the IPO we were a very different company. Most employees were only worried about who was the boss and keeping NTT happy." Now DoCoMo has to worry about its shareholders and bottom line in a far different way.

This certainly reduces the firm's flexibility in some dimensions. And in a company without this inner feeling of strength, we would expect to see managers at many levels becoming less effective as they began looking over their shoulders and managing for shareholder happiness. In DoCoMo, though, we detect something very different. The executives we interviewed have the strength to learn from the implicit and explicit challenges posed by shareholders and financial reporting requirements. For a firm whose success has come from fighting its own corporate and national insularity, this makes the shareholders a major source of value in the ideas and new perspectives that they bring to top management. It's a source DoCoMo can tap into only because it has the feeling of strength.

Challenge Two, Leader Two

Remember, though, that this is a two-front war. Even though DoCoMo is as equipped as any company can be to profit from the sometimes bone-crunching bumps that come with globalization, that might not be enough. Because it's not enough to be fast and successful at expanding the old business; the preceding box on that whiteboard diagram, the one labeled "video," says they also have to change their core business entirely. To be frank, that sounds like a recipe for disaster. For many companies, it would be. But we actually expect DoCoMo to pull this off. The difference, again, is that feeling of strength. It shows a different face, in this battle, and flows mainly from a different leader. But it's the same core passion that, we believe, will propel DoCoMo to a much higher peak.

Bring a New Sense to the Business

Like so many things, the move to "video" seems simple…in concept. Back at the early stage, in the late 1990s, when you're just strategic planners writing boxes on whiteboards, it's the most natural thing in the world to say "and along about 2001, maybe 2002, 3G bandwidth will kick in. That will enable us to offer a whole new level of communication. We'll make even more money." Simple, right? But then, as 2001 stops sounding so far away, you have the working leaders of an active business (some of the same individuals who were strategic planners back then…so there is some justice here…) recognizing the incredible challenge that *all that bandwidth* represents. Because, not only will you have it to offer, so will everyone else. Among other things, that does bad things to the intersection of supply and demand curves for mobile data bandwidth.

So the point isn't just that you'll be able to offer video or other bandwidth-hungry applications; the point is that you *have* to offer them, and somehow get the customers to happily buy, or else you're suddenly a high-quality provider in a commodity business. That leads to epiphanies like Ohboshi's insight about emotional products. It's a great insight, it works well for moving from voice to data, the groundwork is laid, all the preparations are going well, and the same thing should work for the move to 3G, right? But time keeps rolling by, and suddenly even though you're the only country in the world with 3G in actual use, the laggards aren't that far behind. And now it's time to build an active business that somehow fills the "video" box on that old whiteboard. As a company, you've got some reason to be confident; you did it once, developing mobile voice offerings that Japanese customers would actually buy. You did it again, migrating them by the millions from voice to data. But the fact remains, you have to do it again for this mega-bandwidth, 3G world. And that is completely different from anything that DoCoMo has sold in the past. The 3G world is new from the ground up. So the company is once again in completely uncharted territory.

And Shiro Tsuda—a lifelong NTT employee, an engineer who radiates humility, is on point. Tsuda does not fit the Western stereotype of a charismatic leader. Born in Kyoto Prefecture in 1945, he graduated from Keio University with a master's degree in engineering in 1970, and later that same year he joined NTT. He has risen through a number of important posts throughout his career and is currently the executive vice president overseeing the network division. Tsuda's image is far from the flamboyance and individualism so common in U.S. success stories. His path does not echo our caricatures of Bill Gates (rebellious enough to drop out of Harvard and stand up to the U.S. government), or Jobs and Wozniak (with their garage success and high-concept leadership), or even Lee Iacocca (the company man whose greatest success came after the firm he had been loyal to rejected him).

Precisely for this reason, Tsuda is what DoCoMo needs to lead this particular charge. This is the time when quiet, inner strength is absolutely essential. That feeling of strength is vital just to lead the company's 3G efforts through the psychic and intellectual challenge of reinvention. Because, while that is a potentially fatal process, DoCoMo's leaders must approach it—and get others to approach it—as a golden opportunity. They must genuinely have, and then share, the right attitude toward this challenge. As Tsuda told an interviewer, "my personal belief is that success in a particular business field can never last forever. There will be stages of growth, prosperity, and eventually a decline. So, if you want to maintain the prosperity as a company, you have to move on to a new business area continuously." But beyond leadership and courage, DoCoMo's leader in this area needs that feeling of strength because it will turn out to be essential to actually making the 3G strategy happen. To have the vision, to share the vision, then to build the vision—at every level, Tsuda and his team will need strength.

Considering the challenge that 3G represents, for DoCoMo and for the man charged with handling 3G for DoCoMo, it is not surprising to find here a little more humility than top executives typically display. Asked what he would like his personal success story to be after thirty years at NTT and then DoCoMo, Tsuda explains that his personal success story should be the same as the success story of 3G. A humble remark but, on reflection, one that also radiates a feeling of strength.

You see that strength in Tsuda himself. But you also see it in DoCoMo's past behavior. DoCoMo has created unprecedented wealth for its investors, in large part, because the company was extremely skilled at making money from content in a world where content is expensive, risky, and not the forte of large telecomms. When you look closely, the driving passion there was the feeling of strength. And it looks like that passion can be ported directly into the challenge of 3G.

A Content Play

Make no mistake, 3G is a set of technologies. But in the rollout of 3G in Japan and the rest of the world, while technology is important, it won't go anywhere without the content. You need content to use all that bandwidth, to justify it, and to somehow transform it into value that customers will understand, try, and build into their lives. It's like the challenge of creating the killer apps for i-mode, but on a much greater scale. As with i-mode, as with any brand new technology, there will be surprises. No one can really predict which apps will take off when and which fantastically logical candidates will tank.

What DoCoMo does know, though, is that content will be central. Look at the list of areas that Masao Nakamura, head of mobile multimedia, believes will be DoCoMo's future areas of strength:

1. *Location-Based Services:* In cars (multimedia on the move), in navigation services (DoCoMo as information distributor), and in locating services (especially for fleets or delivery).

2. *Information Distribution*: Starting with movie previews and ads, and moving into music, games, and video.

3. *Remote Monitoring or Control Services*: B2B use with inventories of vending machines; already KPN Mobile is starting a service for home/business security and monitoring.

4. *Settlement Business*: Your phone as a credit card—direct access to a bank and ability to pay with the phone.

5. *Convergence of Broadcast and Telecommunication*: Working with broadcasters, cable, digital TV, satellite companies ("nothing specific in mind currently, but taking some stakes in broadcasting").

The potential hazards are clear. Even clearer, though, is the need for a deep feeling of strength. Because all of these applications—and in DoCoMo's view, all possible 3G applications—depend on a successful partnering strategy. Even in the relatively benign environment of its home market, DoCoMo learned early on that there is huge value in being a gentle, nonthreatening partner to content providers. Everyone knows the power of distributors; content providers know it, and resent it, more than most. So if you're successful enough to be an interesting partner to them, and you are offering distribution, you are inherently a threat. You might charge them too much; you might use their content to launch your platform, then replace them; you might partner with their arch-rival, giving that rival a huge competitive edge.

For the distributor, getting past those fears is critical. Not only do you need some content from somewhere but you need it on the right terms, and most importantly, you need it relatively fast. Because you are, remember, in the business of creating demand for a product no one has ever seen. There's a short window of opportunity; miss it, and your technology gets to join DiVx and HomePNA and WebTV and all the other perfectly fine ideas that didn't catch on quickly enough to catch on at all. Being the kind of partner that can get past those fears fast enough, and with enough profit and flexibility to build your business, is an amazing feat. It's what DoCoMo did with i-mode. And it's what requires that profound feeling of strength, the kind that radiates gentle, nonthreatening confidence.

You can hear this brand of strength in Tsuda's words as he modestly explains that Japan is the most advanced country in nonvoice mobile communications—and will obviously be the first major market with 3G capabilities. The strength is clearest in what he doesn't say explicitly:

that DoCoMo is the reason that Japan is so far ahead. Listening to him, you feel there is a strength in this company. A kind, gentle strength.

Gringo Partners

That strength worked incredibly well in recruiting i-mode partners in Japan. It will face a much tougher challenge in the 3G arena—and, let us not forget, in dealing with partners around the world. As Nakamura says, "There are so many personalities and so many companies involved. Technology is not the problem. Everyone understands that and can communicate technically. The difficulty is communicating across industrial and national boundaries." He's talking about challenges like a telecomm working with record companies, bookstores, and publishers, or incumbents who on one hand want to work with DoCoMo, but on the other hand are threatened by the new technology.

And the challenge gets even worse. As Tsuda has pointed out, there are two key issues that will almost surely come up in DoCoMo's 3G negotiations overseas. First, he says, "We must be very careful in vendor selection. Our partners do that now, but we must be more involved. But in terms of the processes themselves, our partners have to do those." Second, he points out, is the special attention that must be paid to the problems of global technology backbones. "In Japan the 3G network is completely new, built from scratch, but in Europe this network will be built on the backbone of the GSM network currently in place."

The Japanese Menace

As if that weren't challenge enough, DoCoMo's global 3G initiative faces an additional barrier: the echoes of Japan, Inc. When Japanese auto, electronics, and steel companies came to share the world markets with U.S. and European firms, there was an inherent "stealth" quality to their rise and positioning in those industries. From the perspective of customers and companies that were accustomed to markets that largely followed national boundaries, these Japanese companies seemed to come from nowhere, vaulting to sudden recognition as true world-class corporations. In at least some cases, the perception of the Japanese entrants—who won market share only after considerable investment, including some false starts—was quite different. Still, while the outside world may see Japan in terms of Toyota- and Sony-style success stories, more recent versions have been rare. DoCoMo is the first Japanese corporation since the 1970s to reach these dizzying heights of global reach and recognition (the one possible exception being the entrepreneurial upstart and holding company, Softbank). Will the world market cooperate in the making of another Japanese giant?

Things are different now, of course. No competitor should count on national boundaries to protect a market. Every businessperson, investor, and government leader is aware that companies are basically transnational. And there are many throughout the Western economies who would be glad to see any improvement in Japan's economy, perhaps even at their own nation's expense, because a healthier Japan will mean a healthier global economy. Yet even so, DoCoMo knows that if it is to succeed with either 3G *or* globalization it must enter foreign markets slowly and carefully, in ways that benefit content providers in that market long term.

Reflecting on these challenges, Tsuda's strength again shows through. While he wants his team to remember that they are doing something no one has done before (and that it will, by definition, be difficult) he also has faith in an organization that has done new things over and over again. "We have started the commercial 3G system this year, and yes, we are the first commercial operators of 3G in the world. But, actually I do not feel any uncertainty about this. The reason I am not concerned is because we already experienced the migration from the first generation, analog, to the second generation, digital, and we've been operating the second-generation system for almost ten years. When we decided to migrate from 2G to 3G, we were able to develop a certain outlook about the future."

This confidence becomes both more credible, and less threatening, when balanced with his obvious awareness of the risks that his business—like your business—must ultimately face. "Since the spin-off from NTT, Tsuda notes that "all of the team members had a determination that we have nowhere to go back to, that we have nowhere to return, so we have to make our own business. Of course we knew the risks, but we overcame those concerns with our determination."

The best way to assess the potential that this quiet feeling of inner strength brings to DoCoMo's future is to look at how well it has worked in the past. As leaders of 3G and Global, respectively, Tsuda and Tsujimura are in the center of one of the key competitive advantages at DoCoMo—the ability to partner and partner well. DoCoMo has few equals, in any industry worldwide, in this skill. The team learned how to partner domestically and eventually became as sharing as anyone in the world. This is more striking than you may realize; Japanese companies are known for total control over their subcontractors. So how did DoCoMo develop such a "giving" attitude?

That attitude flowed from an insight. The insight is that for a firm with the capabilities and weaknesses of DoCoMo, a seemingly generous partnering model is in fact exactly right. Some firms in DoCoMo's position—indeed, several of its competitors worldwide—believe that actually entering the content game, or at least extracting very large rents for distribution, is the obvious way to go. DoCoMo decided early on that such a model would not be sustainable for it. We believe that, paradoxically, it was the company's feeling of strength that allowed it to accurately judge its strategic position. It was strong enough to know its limits.

The Hotel and the Cinema

As a result, DoCoMo was confident enough to reject what Tsujimura calls the hotel model. No, he doesn't mean transient cubicles for a mobile workforce. He's talking about real, physical hotels. The opposite of the hotel model is the cinema model, based on real, physical movie theaters. Between the two, the guy running the hotel has a much more difficult job. He is responsible for figuring out what experience you want; for finding a place to deliver it; for advertising it; for ensuring its consistency; for updating it when your tastes change; and for all the day-to-day work of just plain delivering it.

The owner of a movie theater, in contrast, has a much better deal. His basic responsibility is making sure there's a place, reasonably well located and reasonably well advertised, to see movies. That's it. He does have to run the place efficiently, and consolidation in the U.S. market suggests that margins are thin. But think about what he doesn't have to do. He doesn't have to imagine what kind of movie you might want to see or pay to develop one that might not pay off. He takes a small risk, sure, in screening any given film. But whether it's a turkey or a home run, next week it will be something different. Tastes change, costs of production go up or down—it's largely somebody else's problem. As long as people want to see *something* on a big screen, in a group, with popcorn, he's in business. It's a lot less creative than the hotel business, but also a lot less risky.

When it comes to working with content providers, DoCoMo early on chose to be a cinema, not a hotel. That is, the company acknowledged that, even though it delivered a content product, its business is all about delivery. This took strength, not only to admit the limitations and to turn down the fantasies of capturing all of the content producer's margin, but to let go of so much of "your" product. After all, Sony was in the distribution business for home movies, with Betamax. And it was exactly that fiasco that motivated the founder to take Sony into movies and music; he did not want his company to be at the mercy of content providers.

To put it another way, DoCoMo had the strength to see a huge lesson of the dot-com bubble very early on, and to act accordingly. The lesson? Content may be king, but being king is an expensive and risky business. Because DoCoMo didn't feel the need to own, produce, or fully control the content on i-mode, it has been able to offer the most compelling wireless data product the world has yet seen.

The Economics of Real Strength

Of course, DoCoMo's strength-based partnering strategy meant accepting lower margins. Telia and most other cellular providers in Europe, for example, once charged content providers 50 percent (though they have recently reduced that); NTT DoCoMo has set its level at 7 to 9 percent. Some of its peers feel that's not nearly enough.

And from a "provider" standpoint, it can sound pretty awful; you're still doing all the work of delivering that content, and you're used to taking 100 percent of the fee for data that travels over your network. But DoCoMo understood that the question wasn't revenue, but profits, and that content comes with risk. If you really believe you're going to drive a lot of business through the channel—and if you're going to take only some of the credit risk—then 7 to 9 percent isn't bad. After all, Visa takes just 2 to 3 percent, Amex only 4 percent.

To take a tiny example: If you can count on just 10 percent of your market (say, teenage girls) to download one screensaver a week at one dollar, revenues will be $12 million a month. You only get $800,000 of that, but you don't have to do anything for it. The content creators are plenty motivated to make it work—they maintain the servers, come up with new content, guess the girls' taste, and create the buzz. As the provider, all you do is deliver the bandwidth—whose market price is steadily falling, and which you have to deliver anyway—then sit back and make money.

Overall, DoCoMo's attitude seems to reflect hoary Wall Street wisdom: "The bears make money, the bulls make money, and the hogs get slaughtered." That's an interesting line because, of course, many of us have heard it...yet how many of us have never given in to cross the line into the hogs' category (and later paid for it)? Staying inside your limits takes strength, especially in a booming market.

DoCoMo has displayed that same strength in other domestic partnerships—like the ones with its sales channels, back when it was fighting for retail space. Like the content providers today, those shops were critical to the company's success. And the company believed in its own future enough—had the inner strength—to share generously to ensure that the relationship worked for it. As a result, there is real pride in how the shops look and how they are managed. In the end, that pride paid off for DoCoMo.

A Giant in the Signal

Looking forward, that strength—and the gentle but powerful partnering that results—seems to be even more prominent. Tsuda, for one, sees this willingness to partner with content providers as the whole key to success for i-mode. He made this very clear as he led DoCoMo's 3G initiative.

There must be many opportunities for DoCoMo to simply create some of the content—to fill the pipeline as well as to increase margin. But Tsuda pointed out that if DoCoMo tries to get into the content arena, then "there is a big problem with a giant moving into that space. And if there isn't any content in 3G," he says, "then business won't increase. We need to nurture, facilitate, and work to increase this traffic." That is DoCoMo's main job—and what he has seen as his main responsibility during the three years that he has led this project.

Tsuda, like other key figures throughout DoCoMo, believes in the company's strength—its vision and its capabilities. So he looks at a market challenge that might well be described as frightening and seems to feel only confidence. "In our pursuit of nonvoice communications, what encourages us is the explosive demand for i-mode services and also the fact that the data traffic has been increasing steadily. This justifies that our view for the third generation service is correct."

This same feeling of strength seems to be working its magic on the fears of Japan, Inc. Western executives can never lose sight of the fact that DoCoMo has more experience with the next wave of communications technology than anyone else in the world. And they know, of course, that as technologies are adopted more broadly, the companies with more experience are the ones that usually win. Yet DoCoMo's Western partners, like AT&T Wireless and KPN Mobile, don't seem to feel threatened. They comment on the nonaggressive strength of the DoCoMo executives, with whom they negotiate and work.

Listening to these executives, we are reminded that they (like the leaders of all companies) are individual human beings. They are constantly making judgment calls on how to work with other companies. In the end, those calls boil down to a simple decision: Can we trust these individuals? Do we understand them? Can we work well together? It seems to us that it is DoCoMo's gentle projection of strength, the kind that emanates from Tsuda and Tsujimura, that persuades more and more key partners to say yes.

Afterword

We end, as we began, with a confession: Although we've made some bold predictions in these last few pages about DoCoMo's future...we can't guarantee that we're right. This is real life we're talking about; all sorts of surprising things could happen. And, even if it takes a sudden nosedive, DoCoMo's ultimate trajectory may take years to become clear. As a senior executive frustrated by life inside a large and formerly glorious American automaker told Mitch, "once the firm gets enough scale, the survival space becomes very large." That was his discreet way of saying that, if it's big enough, a company can blunder around, doing all sorts of dumb things, failing at initiative after initiative, and still make money. So we don't know, as we write these last words, whether DoCoMo will live up to the promising future we see deep inside it.

What we do know is that, literally as this book goes to press, a whole variety of external events have begun to fall into place, right where DoCoMo passions have been driving them all along.

■ *Unprecedented growth continues unabated.* In February 2002, the number of total DoCoMo cell phone subscribers crossed the 40 million mark, less than two years after hitting 30 million. Less than two months earlier—the company announced it on Christmas day—

i-mode subscribers had surpassed 30 million. The pure speed and scale are surely remarkable; the company had won 30 million data subscribers in just over one thousand days.

What is even more remarkable, almost shocking, is the sustained pace. Most startups project the infamous hockey stick of growth, with nearly flat progress out to just about the edge of the planning horizon, then a near-vertical rise to market dominance. The last part, seldom graphed, is the return to flat once the market begins to near saturation. DoCoMo's growth puts all that to shame. Up front, it makes the hockey stick look tentative; the i-mode curve looks more like a simple, geometrically perfect mountain, rising at about a 35-degree angle until it literally reaches the heavens. And, at the back end, it doesn't seem to know about saturation. Growth from 20 million to 30 million users took about as long as the rise from zero to 10 million, or from 10 to 20 million. It has started to slow down somewhat, but all the pets and appliances haven't been connected yet.

■ *Success and respect outside Japan are coming just as quickly.* CNN and *Time* magazine designated Keiji Tachikawa, then president and CEO of NTT DoCoMo, as one of the twenty-five most influential executives in the world. *The Economist* noted, as we did earlier, that DoCoMo is the only Japanese firm to make the top ten of Stern Stewart's Wealth Added Index, which ranks the world's 5,069 largest quoted companies by shareholder wealth created (or destroyed) between June 1996 and June 2001. And *Newsweek* called the firm "Japan's only success story," quoting academics who compare it to the Toyotas of the world and even point out that—since it brought the world a new kind of technology, not simply a better example of a familiar one—DoCoMo's achievement may ultimately be even more important.

The company's results have been as impressive as its honors. DoCoMo has recently been listed on both the New York (stock symbol DCM; only the seventeenth Japanese company to achieve that) and London stock exchanges (NDCM)—and announced a five-for-one stock split. The NYSE listing, along with the move of its U.S. headquarters from San Jose to New York, puts DoCoMo much closer to the action outside Japan. And that action is well under way; the company has announced major partnerships with such organizations as Disney, Sun Microsystems, Microsoft, AOL Time Warner, Oracle, IBM, Ericcson, and Nokia.

■ *The global expansion has become visible.* April 2002 brought the news that Bouygues Telecom would license DoCoMo technologies to launch i-mode in France. Only months before, DoCoMo had purchased additional shares of AT&T Wireless, maintaining its 16 percent ownership of the U.S. cellular phone operator even as AT&T Wireless bought the regional cellular phone operator TeleCorp PCS, Inc. Both U.S. and Japanese participants expect the alliance to speeed introduction of 3G wireless and i-mode style wireless multimedia in what should be the world's largest market for wireless data—but one that has been slow to develop. Entry into Taiwan, through partner KG Telecommunications, is expected in mid-2002. (Because of Taiwan's interest in things Japanese, i-mode boasted 10 percent market awareness long before any advertising for the product had started.)

Over in Hong Kong, the DoCoMo stake in Hutchison Whampoa has increased. And under an agreement that covers more than ten years, technology transfer has begun to enable one of DoCoMo's other partners, KPN Mobile, to launch i-mode-like services in the European market. In March 2002, the company announced the launch of i-mode in the Netherlands, Belgium, and Germany. And while spreading i-mode worldwide, DoCoMo is also working globally to cover its flanks. Mindful of Yoshinori Uda's point that Japanese customers need to be able to use their DoCoMo phones worldwide, the company has already begun offering international roaming in Europe, Asia, and Africa.

■ *Technical capabilities continue to lead the global market.* DoCoMo not only is the first company in the world to launch fully commercial 3G services, but also has begun (in April 2002) marketing a 3G terminal with router and hub functions. We're talking about wireless LAN and Web access for PCs, complete with Bluetooth functionality, aimed squarely at small offices, temporary installations, home offices, and the like. Clearly, this is a lot more than a cell phone company. Meanwhile, rollout of FOMA (for "Freedom of Mobile multimedia Access," as DoCoMo calls its 3G service), is proceeding rapidly, with 100,000 subscribers as of April 2002. FOMA is already available in most major Japanese cities and, at current rates, will cover 90 percent of the Japanese population by the end of 2002.

■ *Most important, the killer apps are moving out of the lab and into test markets worldwide.* DoCoMo's single most amazing feat—the one that really hasn't been replicated anywhere else—has been convincing masses of consumers to begin actually using wireless data. It understood sooner, and delivered more fully and aggressively, exactly what Japanese consumers would value from this potentially strange and expensive technology. And the company's passion to replicate that success worldwide is most obvious in its the range and depth of 3G services. As we write, DoCoMo is seriously exploring such applications as:

- *Video*: It is already selling the FOMA D2101V handset, the first in the world equipped for its "i-motion" video-clip transmission service as well as videophone; is delivering movie trailers, music, and similar content; and has begun offering cash prizes to spur development of new video content.

- *Mobile videoconferencing*: Its platform, going into field trials now, shows up to four callers simultaneously on a split screen.

- *Games*: Partnerships are in place with both Sony—those efforts have a strong worldwide emphasis and include DoCoMo partners in Europe and the United States—and Sega, which operates arcade machines throughout Japan.

- *Streaming video advertisements*: Its trial does not even require 3G phones.

- *PDA portal*: It connects browser-equipped PDAs to any DoCoMo phone. Perhaps the experts' vision will finally come to pass...

- *Telematics*: The initial partnership is with Nissan.

- *Camera phone*: In response to J-phone, it features two screens (including one on the outside of the phone so you can see the picture of the person who is calling when the phone rings).

- *Location-based services*: It is widely perceived as the mainstay of mobile commerce and is based on DoCoMo GPS capabilities already launched throughout Japan.

■ *And this generation's Bandai may have emerged.* Perhaps the most frightening candidate for killer app, from the point of view of DoCoMo's competitors, is Cmode. On April 15, 2002, the day that Americans were paying their final taxes for 2001, DoCoMo and its partners Itochu Corporation and Coca-Cola (Japan) announced that this consumer service, which had been operating as a trial in the trendy, youth-centric Shibuya area of Tokyo since autumn of 2001, would be going live all over Japan. At first glance, it's a funky, almost trivial idea—mobile phones and vending machines? Almost as weird as...cartoon screensavers.

Serious analysis of the trials has shown that Cmode has high levels of consumer acceptance—enough that the Coca-Cola Group plans to install Cmode-compatible vending machines called "Cmo" across Japan. Cmo units are equipped with a printer, sensor, and speaker, and are connected to i-mode. "Club Cmode" members use the machines to buy tickets, print coupons, purchase local information such as maps or ringtones, and—of course—buy Cokes. They accumulate user points that can be exchanged for soft drinks or Cmode services; they can also insert cash into the machine to pay for services or increase the credit in their Cmode account.

The program, clearly designed on the basis of real-world experience, gives content providers plenty of incentive to expand the network by installing multiple Cmo machines at their commercial premises, including the opportunity to adapt the Cmo user interface and server system to their needs (for a fee). A combined information kiosk, box office, and vending machine? We admit, it's not the first thing that would leap to our minds, either. But DoCoMo and its partners believe that, for many vendors focused on the youth market, this is a golden customer relationship management (CRM) opportunity.

As for the machine itself, Cmode is just bizarre enough (from the perspective of a grown-up business executive) to appeal to teens. Who knows? It might even be strange enough to spark...love.

Intimacy and M-Commerce
Research Note*

The next wave of economic growth may well depend on a successful move to the wireless Internet economy. With memories of meteoric Internet growth fresh in their minds, companies—particularly in the United States—are rushing to wirelessly enable their e-commerce Web sites. That investment will only make sense if Internet cell phones and similar devices are widely adopted. Only then will they be used for purchases. And our research suggests that cracking the wireless adoption code here in the United States depends on a surprising factor: intimacy.

It's All About People

People won't buy goods and services on wireless devices unless they use those devices heavily. And they won't use them a lot unless they have a compelling personal reason to do so. For many information systems—at the level of the work group, the enterprise, or the market—the first killer app turns out to be simple communication, typically e-mail. Other options sometimes work; VisiCalc, of course, is the

*By Patrick D. Lynch, Accenture Institute for Strategic Change

standard example. But particularly for a technology that is so personal—and so likely to be purchased with personal funds—communication is a much better bet. One look at the modern consumer tells us that people purchase experiences. Experiences are intimate; they happen to us, personally. And they are social; one of the most common ways of enhancing and structuring them is to share them with others we care about. (Just ask any group of friends, at a pub or on a shopping expedition.)

Meet My Friend, the Phone

Mobile data devices can capture this personal quality—the intimacy of ownership and constant contact, the ability to share experiences socially—extremely well. Users in Asia and Europe discovered this early, and the trend continues. According to our recently completed global Harris Poll of more than 3,500 wireless users, 30 percent of U.S. respondents, but more than 50 percent of users from all other countries, use wireless text-based messaging services (e.g., SMS, text chat) to stay in touch with others. This marks a culture of communication and shared personal behaviors around SMS and other wireless techniques not practiced in the United States. More frequently and in different ways, non-U.S. markets use wireless devices to build personal relationships and connect with significant others. Personal identity and social benefits encourage the use of mobile devices for these users; the devices have become extensions of and expressions of the users themselves.

For instance, in Japan twenty-four-hour connectivity makes personal relationships a lot easier to maintain. All of the Japanese respondents interviewed mentioned that because of wireless access they feel more connected to others. They have larger circles of friends and are in contact more frequently with old friends; wireless enables building relationships that they would not have fostered otherwise. Japanese users are accustomed to sending various types of text messages—from meaningless prank messages to trolling for dates to full-blown conversations—at almost every opportunity.

Mobile communications are generally perceived as having improved Japanese relationships with both friends and family. Users reported having more closely-knit and active social lives as a result of these devices.

Finland has also seen the power of wireless devices to enhance personal lives. For many, short text messages are a preferred way to communicate socially. A number of Northern Europeans report that if they have something truly important to say, they like to say it using a short text message. Mobile text messaging offers a way to contact friends and family when they cannot answer their phones—anytime and anywhere, without disturbing others. What's more, the devices themselves have become such a personal form of self-expression that throughout Europe and Asia users accessorize their mobile phones with unique logos, screensavers, and ringtones. It has become so personal that some even report sending graduation party invitations with a mobile phone!

These attitudes translate into heavy use. Worldwide (mostly in Europe and Japan) 15 billion short text messages are sent each month, and 72 percent of Japanese wireless owners use the device to connect to the Internet.

All Work and No Play

Our research found that U.S. users, by contrast, are far less likely to use wireless in ways that foster social relationships. Is it any surprise that, of all the Americans who could use their cell phones or wireless PDAs to access the Internet, only 6 percent actually do so? The relatively low penetration of these devices—roughly a third of the U.S. population versus as much as three-quarters in advanced wireless nations—could make U.S. mobile commerce a nonstarter.

The United States lags in m-commerce because of both adoption and usage. Our research suggests that both problems begin with how Americans view wireless technology: as a purely utilitarian device. Talk to a typical person in the United States about how they use wireless devices and you are likely to hear something about their job. Our poll showed that, compared to their Japanese counterparts, Americans are seven times more likely to use wireless devices to schedule appointments and nearly two and a half times more likely to use them to find business-related information. The difference isn't interest; no one loves business more than the Japanese. Rather the poll results show it is how the wireless device is seen, socially and psychologically.

Making It Personal

Respondents outside the United States have a message for all emerging and future wireless markets that's likely to drive usage up: Consumers need to feel that mobile devices are an extension of themselves. To drive wireless use, you have to engage the user's heart. To do that, consider three ways to make the experience more intimate:

1. **Make wireless less about what users do, and more about who users are.** Mobile devices need accessories, colors, and styles to become a form of self-expression. This is not about which device users buy, but about whether they buy—and use—the device at all. Creating your own "Custom Cover" for the Nokia 5100 phone and the Palm Vx Claudia Schiffer Edition were a step in this direction for U.S. audiences, but other markets are light-years ahead in making wireless devices an extension of themselves. Not only devices, but screens, options, ringtones, and other variables should all be as personalizable and style-oriented as possible. The most successful type of m-commerce application in the world is the mobile phone screensaver in Japan. These color pictures of Hello Kitty, the Bandai Gorilla, or Pokemon personalize phones and become a topic of interest and conversation among friends and business colleagues. It costs approximately 100 yen (less than US$1) to download one of these pictures, and many users change pictures every few weeks. It doesn't take a huge percentage of the almost thirty million i-mode users downloading a screensaver once a month to make this an excellent business proposition.

2. **Leverage voice capabilities, especially for migration.** In contrast to the Europeans and Japanese, U.S. users tend to view text communica-

tion as being somewhat cold. To add warmth, add voice capabilities to the mix—perhaps by providing an instant shift from text to voice communications in the middle of a communication or purchase. To further ease the transition, add data capabilities to voice activities, such as text alerts or responses to voice mails. If you want to encourage mobile phone users to participate in e-commerce on their phones, encourage them to make text-based transactions but give them an easy "off ramp" to an encouraging human being who will answer their questions, become their friend, and then turn them back over to the text system to complete their buys.

3. **Support social connections from the beginning.** This, too, is about making intimacy easier. When wireless subscribers sign up for a service, they do little more than choose the devices and number of minutes they need for access. Many U.S. users may not even realize their mobile device is capable of SMS text messaging. To get the ball rolling, why not dig deeper at the time the service is arranged? Offer to create a network list of social contacts with wireless access and send an initial message to those subscribers (think MCI "Friends and Family" for wireless). One of our Northern European respondents said: "Our youngest child was born last summer and we wanted to deliver the news to almost a hundred people immediately. My husband didn't want to go outside the hospital and make these calls. It was easier to send an SMS message to all. He just selected the numbers from the phone's memory and sent a single message to them all. It was handy."

Spectrum of Utility to Intimacy

Usage rates are not the only challenge for m-commerce; even the Japanese aren't yet purchasing much on their wireless devices. And, once they have become comfortable with the technology, users in the United States could even lead m-commerce. Americans are, after all, a highly mobile population that loves to shop. The utility-focused U.S. view of mobile devices might even connect more quickly to transactions than the pure social view found elsewhere. The rewards for technology companies, content providers, merchants, and consumers would all be substantial. But that is still a little ways down the road; technological history tells us that adoption comes first. And for this technology, in the United States, driving adoption means supporting wireless intimacy.

Interview with Kouji Ohboshi

The Source of a Firm's Vitality Is the Challenge to Create New Markets: Shifting from Volume to Value*

Kouji Ohboshi, president of NTT DoCoMo, the leading mobile phone company that has generated phenomenal growth, talks in this interview about the secrets of creating new markets and his concept for the future mobile business.

Creation of the Mobile Business Leads to Growth in a Firm with 1.2 Trillion Yen in Sales!

Repeated Rate Drops for Users—Direct Communication with Employees

*Nihon Keizal Shinbun, July 19, 1996. Nihon Keizai Shinbun is regarded as the Wall Street Journal of Japan.

What propelled the company into becoming a group corporation with sales of 1.2 trillion yen, triple your level of four years ago?

OHBOSHI: When DoCoMo started its business, the penetration of mobile telephones in the West had already reached 3–7 percent. However, Japan, which was ahead in the world in technology, only enjoyed a market penetration of 1 percent. This figure was surprising, considering the potential demand that should have been bigger. While the economic recession could have been one of the factors for this figure, we discovered another problem that lies with the infrastructure as a result of analysis of customer satisfaction data. While networks of car telephones were constructed in lines alongside roads, mobile phones were used while moving around in a broad area. This reality represented the need to improve the infrastructure, which corresponded to "a plane" rather than "a line."

Preparation of the Infrastructure and Reduction of Fees Are a Corporate Duty

OHBOSHI: Therefore, we made a daring decision to invest tens of billions of yen into infrastructure and working in a plane reconstructed the network to cover Hokkaido through Okinawa. This turned out to be a driving force of rapid growth.

In addition, it was hard to cross "the threshold" of mobile phones due to security money for terminals and subscription fees. This contrasted with the West. When we decided to discontinue the practice of requiring security money, demand tripled in a very short period.

This tripling of demand led to our profits growing. The profits were then injected to reduce charges and in turn stimulated potential demand even further. We considered it our corporate duty to do away with the price gap regardless of competition and to spread mobile communications at an early stage.

Did you expect that the market size would grow like this in four or five years?

OHBOSHI: I gave a lecture at a certain seminar half a year after assuming the post of president. A participant asked what my forecast was for mobile phone demand. The general forecasts at the time were for around 8 million mobile telephones in 2000. However, I replied that we could expect a market of 12.5 million units in 1999 (penetration of 10 percent). Though my figures were reported to be daring, I was confident, as my figures were generated using a growth curve from the West.

However, this number was actually reached three years earlier than I had expected. In addition, we caught up with the U.K. in penetration and our subscriptions became second in the world following the United States.

This was probably due to the rapid change to an information-oriented society and the high economic growth connected with mobility and communication—essential elements of human desire.

Conversations with Employees the Source of His Vitality

You promote direct communication. How does this affect the energy of your company?

OHBOSHI: As the corporation's leader, it is very important to respond quickly to technological innovation and the current situation of rapid growth and changes in the market.

To realize this, I have been proactively trying to remove barriers so that the organization functions promptly and flexibly, and by exchanging and sharing information through direct discussions with employees who are in direct contact with users.

To me, quick decisions are critical. My leaving of the president's office to interact with employees directly has helped me grasp market trends promptly and respond in a timely fashion.

Such direct communication also serves to encourage employees by sending messages such as, "Do not solely rely on the company," and "Independence and originality make you realize the significance of your existence. Please live life to the fullest."

Why does DoCoMo need to be multicultural?

OHBOSHI: As the Company was spun off from NTT, people with various experiences and skills work for the company. In addition, we are recently proactively promoting the hiring of mid-career employees and temporary workers to full-time employees as well as foreign workers. These facts make it difficult to have a single corporate culture.

I expect that weaving multiple cultures of unique people with various experiences and different values will generate corporate dynamism.

Breakthrough in the Accepted in Mobile Communications Creating New Markets Through Nonvoice Services from 9.6 kilobits to 28.8 kilobits

What is the background behind proposing the new concept of "from volume to value?"

OHBOSHI: Sales have grown as if it was a doubling game up until now. However, in forecasting the future I was forced to conclude that volume-oriented management would not continue to work for long. The market will be saturated earlier than we expected. Therefore we have to be prepared by converting our management strategy from one focused on quantity to one seeking to improve quality including the developing of applications.

If we neglect possible new challenges, we tend to rest on past success and to be conservative. This is dangerous.

What is the stage of the digital communication network's infrastructure?

OHBOSHI: Though nonvoice service at present accounts for approximately 1 to 2 percent of communication traffic, we hope to make it grow to over 10 percent in four to five years. To realize that, we need to increase the speed of the data transmission infrastructure, including the transmission of image information. In 1995, the speed of digital networks increased to 9.6 kilobits per second from 2.4 kilobits. It will jump to 28.8 kilobits, or a speed three times faster, to start packet communications in March 1997. This completed compatibility with mobile computing including satellite mobile communications.

However, compatibility with mobile multimedia requires a faster access speed in the mega range via a different method from the conventional method. Consequently, we plan to begin testing a new method this fall.

Satellite mobile communications will be applied more to non-voice service such as data transmission in addition to expansion of the maritime communications area (from 50 kilometers offshore to 370 kilometers); monitoring systems for roads and rivers that also serve as measures for dealing with disasters; image transmission for ecological observations; simultaneously transmitting identical information from a single location to several spots; and measures for sending information to remote areas.

Concept of Mobile Phones Undergoes Total Change

Do you think that the high-speed digital communications networks will totally change the concept of mobile phones?
OHBOSHI: Yes, I do. High-speed data transmission service will diversify the way mobile telephones are used in one step. Usage of data transmission and facsimile transmission has started increasing already. Karaoke on demand using mobile telephones and use of the Internet via mobile telephones has also started.

As a result, use of the mobile telephone network in nonvoice fields, which has been dominantly used for voice fields, should grow in leaps and bounds.

The reason why nonvoice use has not grown so far lay with its charge system and communication speed. The monitor test showed us that a charge of 20 yen per minute would be practical. In addition, realization of packet communications will make it possible to reduce the charge even further through a charge system based on quantity of information.

The FLEX-TD pager system will allow transmission of seventy letters on average. This means that a pretty significant amount of information can be transmitted. There is a possibility that it will be used for PDAs (personal digital assistants), and it is being developed currently.

Do users support the competitiveness of DoCoMo in a very competitive industry?

OHBOSHI: A market study on mobile telephones conducted in November 1995 asked why they had chosen DoCoMo. The top three responses were: "The service area is far greater than others," "The quality is excellent," and "Good postsales service is available nationwide." The response, "Can be used for data transmission" was ranked 4th and was given by 14 percent of the respondents.

This figure reveals a large latent need for nonvoice services as well as big expectations for DoCoMo.

Responsibility of DoCoMo to Meet the Borderless Age

How do you plan to promote third-generation mobile communications?
OHBOSHI: We have been approaching the third-generation system in cooperation with related government ministries and agencies as well as other companies. However, it should not be realized with the exclusion of foreign countries. From the very beginning, we have suggested open joint research projects. We have a plan to develop it in cooperation with major countries in Asia, the United States, and Europe.

What is the real situation of internationalization?
OHBOSHI: DoCoMo's research institutes are open to overseas technical experts and researchers. We would like to improve the efficiency and speed of research and development by using each other's technology.

Globalization first requires proactive acceptance of overseas trainees. We accepted about 150 trainees from forty countries in 1995, and more people will be accepted this year.

Another important thing is to proactively introduce networks or terminals from overseas if they are good. Products from about ten overseas companies are procured at present.

How about dealing with social responsibility of the company and support for welfare work?
OHBOSHI: Although diffusion of mobile phones should be welcomed, it is disappointing that a new social problem has occurred with that.

We are actively conducting a campaign to prevent dangerous situations by asking users to refrain from talking over mobile telephones in places where many people gather, including inside trains and restaurants, and also asking people to pull cars over before talking on the phone. In addition, to prevent troubles with electronic medical equipment caused by use of mobile telephones in hospitals, the company has been proactively cooperating with concerned groups and specialists to set up guidelines.

Company's Raison d'Etre

OHBOSHI: Furthermore, a part of profits was donated in fiscal 1995 to a social welfare conference operating in ten prefectures that were our business area. We plan to continue this form of support. Regarding the promotion of academic research in communication technology, we gave donations to four national and private universities. We are planning to provide donations to more universities next fiscal year.

We established the Social Environment Division this year and employees involved in volunteer activities are gaining the backing of the company. Campaigns for collecting and recycling used batteries for mobile telephones are being conducted as measures to protect the environment.

As for cultural activities, a "DoCoMo concert" is held once a month at the terrace on the first basement floor of the company's headquarters. Donations are also given to two music colleges cooperating with the company to assist the young.

Your company seems to be conducting valuable activities for contributing to society. What is the philosophy behind those activities?
OHBOSHI: When a company grows, its relationship with society deepens. Therefore, it is only natural to utilize a company's administrative resources for purposes other than primary business, as it is a member of society. We should not forget that companies would not develop without a healthy development of the society. I think taking a big role in such activities as well as contributing to the development of society through provision of mobile communications is our company's raison

d'etre. I also would like the employees to be "interested in society" and be "caring people," while their own company is growing.

INDEX